Also by Arlene Modica Matthews

Why Did I Marry You, Anyway?

Your Money, Your Self

•

Understanding and Improving

Your Relationship to Cash and Credit

Arlene Modica Matthews

A Fireside Book

PUBLISHED BY SIMON & SCHUSTER

NEW YORK · LONDON · TORONTO

SYDNEY · TOKYO · SINGAPORE

FIRESIDE

Simon & Schuster Building
Rockefeller Center
1230 Avenue of the Americas
New York, New York 10020

First Fireside Edition 1993

FIRESIDE and colophon are registered trademarks
of Simon & Schuster Inc.

Designed by Laurie Jewell
Manufactured in the United States of America

1   3   5   7   9   10   8   6   4   2

Library of Congress Cataloging-in-Publication Data is available.

ISBN 0-671-68278-4
ISBN: 0-671-78913-9 (PBK)

Acknowledgments

I AM INDEBTED to the many people who shared with me their thoughts and feelings on the subject of money and to those who offered their professional opinions on money's psychology. Among the latter group I would especially like to acknowledge Arch Crawford, David Dreman, Dr. David Forrest, Dr. Sheila Klebanow, Michael Linton, Dr. Eugene Lowenkopf, Dr. Byron Miller, Bill Morelli, Jim Polos, Dr. Ann Ruth Turkel, and Patrick Waide.

I am grateful to my editor, Bob Asahina, and my agent, Bob Tabian, for their valuable ideas and unfailing encouragement; to Laura Yorke for the meticulous attention she paid to this manuscript in each of its incarnations; and to my research assistant, Lori Lynn Bauer, for enriching this project with her diligence and enthusiasm.

I remain, as always, thankful to the many friends who valiantly endured my obsessiveness as this book took shape. And once again I thank Claudia Goodman and Greg Peters for offering the emotional and geographic sanctuary of which I so shamelessly availed myself. Lastly, I would like to thank the trustworthy, loyal, helpful, friendly, courteous, kind, cheerful, and brave (etcetera) Gary Uhl without whose abundant "good turns" I might never have made it through.

For Barry Ivan

Contents

Throughout this book, the use of the pronoun "he," when used generically, is meant to convey "he or she." "His" is meant to convey "his or hers."

1
PART

- - - - - - - - - -

Mad About
Money

- - - - - - - - - -

A Stream
of Money

. . . .

JOHN KENNETH GALBRAITH has written, "The pursuit of money, or any enduring association with it, is capable of inducing not alone bizarre, but ripely perverse behavior." Since most of us are wont to pursue money to some extent, and since, in order to function in daily life, we must have an enduring association with it, does it follow that all of us exhibit at times certain money-related behaviors that are somewhat peculiar, downright outlandish, or perhaps even flagrantly absurd?

It certainly appears so.

Many people seem to have a ready anecdote about a friend, relation, or colleague they feel harbors a touch—or more—of money madness. On further reflection, they're even apt to admit that, yes, they are prone to a trace—or more—of it themselves.

Indeed, the world seems to be teeming with people who routinely spend money they do not have, or who feel compelled to count pennies when there is no practical need to scrimp, or who forfeit life's pleasures to chase ceaselessly after lucre, or who repeatedly find that bitter disagreements about money strain their friendships, their marriages, and their bonds with family members. It is filled, too, with sophisticated people who, despite their savvy, repeatedly make investments in schemes doomed to fail, with talented people who cannot seem to manage to translate their skills into an adequate income, and with responsible people who despite their usual attentiveness to detail go out of their way to avoid coping with issues of finance. When it comes to money matters, their foresight, insight, judgment, and discrimination seem to vanish as surely as if someone had taken a chisel to their frontal lobes.

Yet such people would hardly qualify as lunatics. They are ordinary humans who, for reasons this book will attempt to illuminate, became highly susceptible to money's propensity to overpower, frighten, awe, seduce, infuriate, and confuse. They are people whose relationship to money is informed by an attitude—or combination of attitudes—that frequently results not only in harm to their pocketbooks, but in harm to their self-image and spirit, as well as harm to their ability to find fulfillment in their work and in their personal relationships.

Indeed, "they" are none other than "we." For, to some degree, most of us harbor irrational attitudes toward money.

If we lived on "Star Trek" 's planet of Vulcan, a place where logic conquers all and where emotions exert no unruly tug on thought and on behavior, we would probably live thoroughly consistent and exquisitely well-balanced pecuniary lives. Where money was concerned, we would be able to give ourselves reasonable orders and follow them to the letter: Earn more. Spend less. Budget. Save for retirement. Pay estimated tax on time. Buy low, sell high. Go ahead and ask for that raise. Use your money to protect yourself and pleasure yourself. Share it with those you love—and, to the best of your ability, with those who need it. Above all, don't let it make you crazy.

Here on Earth, however, each of us seems to be endowed with a Money Complex—an intertwined group of psychical "weak spots" that, in various circumstances and in response to various emotional triggers, erupt into seemingly nonsensical behavioral symptoms. This book is about how that Money Complex is formed, layer upon layer, from infancy through adulthood. It is a book about the evolution of money attitudes. And it seeks to show how irrational money attitudes—which in large part lurk in the realm of the unconscious—can be transformed into more rational ones by being brought into the light of conscious awareness.

In my work as a psychotherapist I have seen over and over again how coming to terms with one's Money Complex can yield profound results that resonate in realms far beyond the financial. For our money attitudes are not isolated psychic phenomena but an integral part of who we are. As we shall see, they are shaped by many factors, influenced by many variables over the course of many years. And as they are shaped, they in turn shape us, reflecting how we treat ourselves and others and, not infrequently, serving as a kind of magnifying mirror for other facets of our personality.

Consequently, someone who is able to understand why he is withholding with money may learn a thing or two about his tendencies to withhold, say, praise or affection or effort or information from those with whom he lives and works. Someone who is able to understand why he is perennially anxious about his financial status may learn something about his self-esteem, his envy, or his fear of dependency. Someone who is forever managing to impoverish himself financially may come to terms with why he is bent on self-sabotage, and perhaps even how he may begin to reverse his overall self-destructive bent.

What's more, in beginning to understand the sources of one's own money quirks, one can better understand the heretofore incomprehensible money-related behavior of the people who impact on one's life—both at home and in the workplace. Suddenly, communication may be easier, compromise and cooperation more achievable, disagreements less destructive. For we will be able to separate actual money issues from interpersonal emotional issues with which they may have been getting confused.

Along with all these benefits, those who come to understand the sources of their own money madness will doubtless enjoy greater financial freedom—in the largest sense of the term. They may be able to save more than ever before; or if they lacked the courage to spend, they may be freed up to indulge themselves in some small luxuries that are indeed within their grasp. They may be able to earn more than ever before; or if in the past they found themselves working at a joyless job for the sake of money alone, they may be freed to work more happily at a different and more pleasing job while earning a little less. They may be able to give a little more; or if they found themselves giving more than they could actually spare out of guilt or shame or the fear that others might love them less if they were not plied with money, they may be freed to say, "Enough is enough."

This book is not a career or investment guide. It will not offer specific suggestions on how to make money or make your money grow. However, if aspects of your money attitudes are preventing you from having a sufficient amount of it, you may discover that and begin to change.

This book is not a moral treatise about how "wicked" it is to be concerned about money, nor a rah-rah money-is-great-and-anyone-can-make-a-bunch inspirational guide. But if aspects of your money attitudes are compelling you to ignore financial concerns when there is a pressing need to address them, or, conversely, to obsess on pecuniary matters to the exclusion of most other things, this book could help you discover these behavior patterns and begin to change them.

The changes you experience, however, are not likely to be one-shot revisions or narrow course corrections. They are, instead, likely to lead to other changes—and then to others still.

It is from the Latin word *moneta* that the word "money" was born. The first Roman coins were struck at the temple of the goddess Juno Moneta, or Juno the Warner, who was worshipped for her wise counsel and her ability to foresee the future. But *moneta* grew from an even older word, *moneo*, which means not only "to warn" but also "to teach."

Money has much to teach us, though learning its lessons is not always easy. In daily life we are caught up in a stream of money, like trout in a stream of water. Alas, what surrounds us is often the last thing we can clearly see.

1

. . . .

Money
Meanings,
Moods, and
Maladies

. . . .

Let us define money as that which possibilizes the imagination.

—JAMES HILLMAN

Money is the MOMENT to me.
Money is my MOOD.

—ANDY WARHOL

AT THE ENTRANCE to the visitors' gallery of the Bureau of Printing and Engraving in Washington, D.C., a sign says, "The buck starts here." From a perch overlooking a quartet of multivalved rotary presses one can witness the high-speed printing, dyeing, drying, proofreading, and trimming of a million dollars' worth of currency every twenty minutes. By 2 P.M., Monday through Friday, all tourists are obliged to leave, but the presses continue to roll. Seven days a week, all day long, the crisp new bills of cotton and linen are produced. All night, too. Tomorrow when we wake, there will be row upon row of them, as fresh and reassuring as breakfast muffins lined up in their tins. Baked while you sleep.

On the trading floor of a major commercial banking firm, money is also being made. Ardent and frantic twenty-five-year-olds, speculating in the foreign exchange futures and op-

tions markets, are haggling urgently. They shout, "Mine, mine!" to indicate a buy and "Yours, yours!" to solidify a sell. They man telephones, monitor computer screens, and keep one ear to the ground, ever sensitive to news leaks, political rumors, economic gambits, and the good old-fashioned gossip that fuels the fires of collective greed and fear and determines the "value" of the dollar.

At a New Age Prosperity Workshop, in a room lit by candles and perfumed with incense, participants following the instructions of a "financial healer" anoint "sacred" dollar bills with patchouli oils, fold them into tiny pyramids, and tuck them beneath a weighty crystal. After a series of rituals and prayers, they place their dollars back into their wallets, where, aided by the faith and energy of their bearers, they are expected forthwith to muliply like randy bunnies.

At the New York Stock Exchange, a building whose ponderous façade is modeled after a Roman temple, green blips representing money flash across a giant screen. Yet even as hundreds of scurrying workers steal furtive glances at money's abstract representation, tangible money is arriving by the truckload at the New York Federal Reserve Bank two blocks to the north. Inside the bank, behind the elaborate wrought-iron gates of a structure meant to mimic a Florentine Renaissance palace, tens of millions of dollars in cash are fed each day into enormous sorting machines where "fitness detectors" sift apart reusable currency from worn, torn, and soiled bills. The money that cannot be recirculated is promptly shredded into oblivion.

Observing the shredding process from behind the thick glass walls toward which their tour guide has escorted them, an awestruck family stands in silence. At last the father turns to his little boy and girl and whispers softly. "It's all right," he tells them. "You see, it's only paper."

. . . .

What is money, anyhow? It is a medium of exchange and a store of wealth. It is a convenient artifact used to procure goods and services, the ultimate practical necessity. Small wonder that when Woody Allen awakens from a two-hundred-year nap in *Sleeper*, his immediate concerns are that his rent is more than two thousand months past due and that his Polaroid stock, purchased at seven dollars a share, is probably worth millions. The maxim that "money sets all the world in motion" will doubtless be as true in the twenty-second century as it was in 42 B.C., when Pubilius Syrus first uttered it.

Money is also a unit of measure—like an inch or a pint, a degree or an ounce—on which everyone in a given society agrees. If I give you ten dollars, you know as well as I that it can be used to purchase ten dollars' worth of groceries or two five-dollar train tickets. But if it's a twenty-dollar haircut you're after, you will need twice as much. Simple.

Yet if what money measures at the grocery store or the barbershop is relatively simple, what it measures in the mind is a far more complicated matter. Indeed, it is impossible to truly comprehend what money *is* without understanding what it means. And yet, how could it be possible to make blanket statements about the meaning of money? To a great extent, money's meaning, like that of a Rorschach ink blob, is in the mind of the beholder.

In her novel *The Accidental Tourist*, Anne Tyler described a character who thought of money as "something almost chemical—a volatile substance that reacted in various interesting ways when combined with other substances." In the deepest recesses of the mind, money indeed combines with other "substances." It intermingles with fantasies, fears, and wishes and blends with a grab bag full of blind spots, embellishments, denials, distortions, impulses (e.g., "I want it! I want it!"), and defenses against those impulses (e.g., "But I don't want to *look* like I want it."). Such combinations result in money undergoing the sort of symbolic displacements that occur in dream life, where one object may often stand for another object or even represent the tangible embodiment of an emotion.

Many of us make subjective emotional associations to money. Among the myriad things money can signify are armor, ardor, admiration, freedom, power and authority, excitement and elation, insulation, survival and security, sexual potency, victory and reward.

The associations we make to something affect how we perceive it. Thus, money may be perceived as a weapon or a shield, a sedative or a stimulant, a talisman or an aphrodisiac, a satisfying morsel of food or a warm fuzzy blanket.

Furthermore, the associations and perceptions we make with regards to any object naturally give us a constellation of feelings about its presence or absence. So having money in our pockets, to save or to spend, may provide us with feelings of fullness, warmth, pride, sexual attractiveness, invulnerability, perhaps even immortality. Similarly, experiencing a dearth of money may bring on feelings of emptiness, abandonment, diminishment, vulnerability, inferiority, impotency, anxiety, anger, and envy.

Some studies have borne out the fact that an "injection" of money, even a tiny one, may serve as a mood elevator as powerful as any drug, prompting cheer and goodwill toward one's fellow men. In one study, a team of University of Pennsylvania psychologists arranged for unwitting subjects to "find" ten cents in the coin-return slot of a public telephone. Eighty-eight percent of those subjects were willing immediately afterward to assist an unknown woman (in actuality a colleague of the experimenters) who had "dropped" a manila folder and scattered papers on the ground. Of the control group that did not find a dime, only 4 percent were equally magnanimous.

Other studies have borne out the fact that monetary deprivation can induce or contribute to mental depression. A Gallup survey, for example, concluded that women with household incomes over $50,000 generally reported fewer bouts of depression than women with household incomes under $20,000.

If a perennial lack of money can bring on gloom, it should come as no shock that a sudden money loss can—quite literally—bring on doom. At the onset of America's Great Depression in 1929, a plethora of ruined investors who could not meet the margin calls on their plummeting stock themselves plummeted from the windows of Wall Street. When a West German investment adviser realized his mistake in selling short during the surging bull market of the mid-1980s, he, too, committed suicide, leaving a note that read, "I announce to you full of pain and shame, the total loss of security deposits managed by me."

Yet when it comes to money, cause and effect are not always so obviously linked, and the relationship of mood to money is not always what one might expect. For example, though depression is *often* associated with the loss of money and euphoria with its gain, such is not always the case. In a seeming paradox, an influx of money for some can instigate negative feelings, from disappointment and disillusionment to guilt and shame. Studies have also shown that a significant number of large jackpot lottery winners experience lethargy, a sense of purposelessness, and sometimes even despair once they have their winnings in hand. Though one might expect them to be kicking up their heels for a rousing chorus of "We're in the Money," they are more likely to be found desultorily watching hour upon hour of television. Financial depletion, on the other hand, may provide some people positive feelings, like those of self-righteousness, virtue, and superiority. The potential for such feelings exists because, to *some* minds at some times, money may signify secrecy, silence, trickery, tedium, or outright terror. It may be associated with something taboo, something dangerous, or something demeaning. It may be perceived not as food but as filth, not as a comfort but as a burden, not as sacred but as profane, not as empowering but as overwhelming, not as something to be sought but rather as something to be shunned.

It may seem strange that money, which unarguably can provide us with many of life's pleasures—not to mention basic necessities—does not hold a consistently positive value. But if we want verification that money causes many idiosyncratic and inconsistent thoughts, perceptions, and feelings, we need only remember all the instances we've witnessed of idiosyncratic and inconsistent money-related behavior. And we need only understand that all too often money behavior is based not on reason but on attitude and emotion. If one observes behavior and applies deduction, one can often ascertain the underlying associations and feelings that created it.

But why are there so many different types of strange behavior when it comes to money? Why do certain people seem to go out of their way to sabotage their financial health, while others sacrifice the very pleasures money can buy simply to spend all their time accruing more and more of it? And why do so many people seem to vacillate between attempting to acquire money and attempting to rid themselves of it?

Because people have vastly different emotional makeups. And because each human personality incarnates money in its own way, imprinting it with a personal psychic stamp.

THE MONEY PERSONALITY

From time to time, one runs across quizzes in popular magazines that purport to be able to discern one's financial "personality" by asking "What would you do if you won a million dollars?" "Would you lend money to your best friend for a shaky investment?" "Do you tip as much for good service as for poor?" "Can you resist that 'perfect' item of clothing that simply costs too much?"

But those of us who have obediently checked off multiple-choice responses whenever such a challenge presented itself may well have noticed that we are often tempted to pencil in the nonexistent category "All of the Above."

We'd like to (a) spend the mythical million dollars on suntan lotion in Bora Bora *and* (b) give it to our aging parents *and* (c) save it for our growing children *and* (d) invest it in T-bills (or mutual funds or gold or guava juice futures). We'd like to turn our best friend down, talk sense into him, give him a little money, give him everything we've got because, hey, we're the kind of people that value friendship more than cash. The options unroll before us and around us like a lush pinwheel of endless red carpets and our minds get dizzy with prospects. Are we (a) Money Wasters, (b) Money Chasers, (c) Money Avoiders, (d) Money Prudes, (e) Money Midases?

Our unruly answers refuse to fit into neat columns. We want to do all of the above because, to different degrees and in response to different stimuli and situations, we may *be* all of the above.

A person's money personality is not unlike his overall personality. It is part primal id, seeking only pleasure and relief from tension, driven by impulse and a longing for immediate gratification. It is part superego or "conscience," influenced by countless constraints and internalized "should" and "shouldn't" commands imparted by society and by significant people in our lives, prone sometimes to constructive self-corrective guilt, sometimes to relentless destructive self-punishment.

When we take action with money, we may sometimes be acting on behalf of what our superego deems the Good Self—perhaps the Virtuous Scrimper, the Exceedingly Generous Charitable Donor, the Hypercautious Investor, or the Vigilant Bargain Hunter. We may sometimes be acting on behalf of what it deems the Bad Self—perhaps the Unlucky Gambler, the Chronic Borrower, or the Corner-Cutting Petty Cheat. We sometimes act on behalf of the id, behaving in ways we deem so impulsive and "uncharacteristic" that they are part of what we perceive as our Non-Self. We may engage in spur-of-the-moment extravagances in a kind of fugue state and later feel like comedian Flip Wilson's mischievous character Geraldine, who plaintively contended, "The *devil* made me buy that dress."

But our money personality is also part reasonable and logical conscious ego, attempting—sometimes successfully, sometimes futilely—to rationally mediate between the two psychic polarities of id and superego and between the requirements of internal and external pressures (say, our genuine physical and mental need for a week's vacation versus our practical need to preserve what's left of our sagging checkbook balance). The ability to calculate, weigh all reasonable alternatives, inhibit impulses, and reflect before acting where money is concerned is a hallmark of healthy ego functioning. Yet it is no easy task for anyone's ego to stay on top of money matters.

Id and superego voices resonate loudly in the psyche, oftentimes tending to drown out the voice of reason. Consequently, as Norman O. Brown writes in *Life Against Death,* "We are all neurotic. . . . Between 'normality' and 'abnormality' there is no qualitative difference, but only a quantitative difference." Money serves as the perfect blank screen onto which human neurosis may project itself. Thus most people, no matter who they are or how much money they have, no matter what their gender or social class or cultural background, have some sort of Money Complex.

If we hope to explain what seems inexplicable in our own behavior, if we hope to lessen the effects of the Money Complex and to reduce the level of money neurosis in our own lives, we must set ourselves a task. We must become more aware of what money means to us on various levels, observe the connection between our feelings and our financial motivations, and realize when our subliminal unconscious "voices" are speaking. Then, rather than heeding these voices blindly, we may filter them through our conscious mind and make a more analytic, well-informed decision as to what to do about getting, spending, earning, enjoying, saving, or sharing money.

If, for example, we are feeling anxious about whether or not we have enough money, and we give in to the feeling without examining its source, we will likely repeat whatever behavior we have engaged in in the past when in the throes of such an emotion. We may take on an extra job and eat nothing but macaroni and cheese. We may pore laboriously over our accounts in the hopes that newfound funds will miraculously materialize. We may call our parents and plead for a loan. We may cast about for a get-rich-quick scheme. We may even brandish our credit cards and spend to the limit in an act of frustration and hopelessness that says, in effect, "If I'm going to go broke anyhow, I may as well do it right."

If we examine the anxious feeling, however, we may learn whether the monetary danger we face is a danger from without, i.e., based on real circumstances in the real world, or whether it is a peril manufactured within our own psyche.

Perhaps the anxiety is springing from our own hidden impulses, and what we fear is our own tendency to spend profligately at the slightest provocation. Perhaps the anxiety is springing from an internalized parental authority figure that has conditioned us to call home, hat in hand, at periodic intervals to renew the family bond. Perhaps we are responding to social pressures that induce in us the conviction that unless we have more money we will face ostracism within our particular community.

If upon sober reflection we determine that our anxiety is reality-based and that we indeed do *not* have enough money at hand to meet a pressing expense, we can then decide how best to increase our income or decrease our outgo. If, on the other hand, we are able to ascertain that our peril is primarily "in our head," we may be able to forestall our rote responses to anxiety and spare ourselves a good deal of unnecessary grief in the bargain.

A SPECTRUM OF MONEY MADNESS

Certainly, unreasonable behaviors regarding money span a continuum. The degree to which people react neurotically to money will vary, with the reactions of some being far more acute than the reactions of others. At the lower end of the spectrum are mild eccentricities and subtle symptoms—a little thoughtless action now and again, perhaps a wee bit of chintziness—the results of which seem relatively benign. The behaviors in which mild money madness manifests itself may not prove overly annoying or frustrating to people who engage in them. More likely they are apt to annoy and frustrate those who *interact* with people who engage in them. Certainly no irreparable harm will occur as the result of a tendency to undertip doormen and mail carriers at Christmas—except, of course, to doormen and mail carriers.

At the mid-range of the continuum are moderate money neuroses. Here we find people who are somewhat too easily parted with their money, somewhat too preoccupied with making it, or somewhat too bent on hanging on to it. Some of these moderate neuroses tend to be overlooked more than they should. Indeed, some are deemed socially praiseworthy, e.g., a tendency to overgive to charity even when it stretches one's personal budget. And some are deemed economically useful, e.g., a tendency toward overwork purely for monetary gain. But those who exhibit them are likely bound to suffer sooner or later, if not in their pocketbooks then in other areas.

As one moves higher up the continuum, money madness is capable of wreaking all manner of havoc, both on financial and emotional planes. Severe money maladies frequently interfere with people's ability to experience pleasure or to function effectively in the world. For where a preoccupation with, say, asset accrual or financial prophylaxis is close to all-consuming, there is precious little psychic energy left over for anything else.

Where severe money maladies are present, it is because a particular id-based or superego-based irrational emotional association—or group of associations—to money looms especially large in the psyche. Those associations may be reflections of overall character bents (e.g., a controlling person will associate money with something that must be tightly controlled and approach it with the same fastidiousness with which he approaches, say, his diet, his daily schedule, or his hygienic habits). They may reflect skewed emotional messages learned in the bosom of one's family (e.g., "Money is love"). They may stem from a pronounced susceptibility to a particular money message that permeates one's cultural milieu (e.g., "Conspicuous consumption is the key to happiness"). Or they may be the result of some combination of these factors. Whatever their genesis, these irrational associations tend to blossom into full-fledged irrational money attitudes. And these irrational attitudes tend to result in action which is baffling to behold—and which often can prove debilitating in many facets of one's life.

When, for example, people equate money with something taboo, they often assume an attitude of clandestineness toward it. They may portray themselves as having very little money, even if they have a good deal of it. And they may take great pains and endure great deprivation to squirrel money away. A young man recalls:

> Sometimes we'd visit my grandmother at night, and the only light in her whole house would be the glow from the television screen—a black-and-white portable TV. If you switched on a lamp, she'd come up behind you and switch it back off. Though she and my grandfather had worked more or less incessantly in their tailor shop all their lives, she insisted they'd never made a profit. For forty-five years she had lived in a pretty bad neighborhood in the same run-down apartment, never spending on anything but bare necessities. And she refused to take money from her children. Then she died, leaving over a quarter of a million dollars in a passbook savings account to be divided among six grandchildren. The whole family was blown away when the will was read. We never had a clue.

When people perceive and use money as armor and insulation, they may assume a paranoid stance with regard to it. They may live in fear that others will try to part them from their "wealth."

Miss A., a patient in therapy, diligently avoided intimate relationships with men. Convinced that any man who so much as glanced at her would doubtless try to marry her for the inheritance left her by her grandfather, she began to dress in a manner that masked her physical attractiveness and to cloister herself at home in an attempt to avoid "fortune hunters." Finally her therapist could no longer stand the suspense. He asked how much her inheritance was actually worth. It turned out to be a moderate sum indeed, hardly enough to entice a self-respecting gigolo.

When people equate money with affection, they may assume a tit-for-tat attitude toward it. They often use money as a vehicle for quid pro quo emotional exchange. One woman confides:

Things weren't going so well between me and the man I'd been seeing. I must admit it was partly because his penny-pinching got on my nerves. One night during dinner in a restaurant, we had a quarrel and I began to feel it was pointless to continue the relationship. Later, at my apartment, I told him so. He seemed to take it well at the time. A few days later I received what looked like an invoice. He had broken down the cost of our last evening together—meal, tip, cab fares—and said I owed him half. It was seventeen dollars. I sent it to him in rolls of pennies.

When people associate money with admiration, their self-esteem quotient can become inexorably linked to the amount of money they have, or imagine they will have. They may assume a symbiotic attitude toward money and become entirely dependent on it to bolster a fragile sense of self.

Mr. B., another therapy patient, boasted all his life of the large inheritance he believed he would have from his Aunt Martha. When Aunt Martha finally passed on at ninety-five, it became clear, as Mr. B. said forlornly, that she had been "eating principal for breakfast, lunch, and dinner." His inheritance consisted solely of several threadbare Oriental rugs. Mr. B.'s inflated ideas about his future came to an abrupt halt, and his self-esteem plummeted accordingly. Among other things, he managed to lose his job and gain fifty pounds within a year of his aunt's demise.

On a pragmatic ego-oriented level, money certainly translates into survival and security. Yet when people overassociate it with these things, they may assume an attitude of high anxiety toward money. They can become bent on controlling money, on fiercely guarding it, lest it somehow disappear. But in attempting to be money's master, they may become its slave. A bemused gentleman recalls:

Last summer my parents, my wife, and I took a trip to the town in Sicily where my father was born. While there, we met two of his brothers, who took turns feting us in their homes. After a few days, my wife and I planned to leave to visit Agrigento and see the temples there. One of my uncles told my father he was upset because my wife and I had not had as many meals with them as we had with my other uncle. I asked my father to extend an invitation to my uncle, his wife, and son. "Ask them to come to our hotel in the morning," I said, "and we can all have breakfast together before we leave." My father said that would be impossible. "They can't come to the hotel," he explained, "because they can't all leave the house at the same time." I asked him why not. "Because someone has to stay home with the money." It turned out that my uncle's family had no faith in banks and kept their life savings in a chest under the bed. They never left it unguarded.

When people see money as something confusing and frightening, they may assume an attitude of helplessness with regard to it (indeed, they may use money to express an overall helpless stance). Often they would far more willingly surrender money than engage in any kind of confrontation about it, especially when the confrontation is with an authority or a bureaucracy. A frustrated daughter says:

My parents took a cross-country driving vacation, and my mother asked me to make their arrangements, which I did. I instructed her to send a check to my travel agent, who would make hotel and rental-car deposits in advance. When a duplicate car-rental charge showed up on my mother's credit card—obviously an error—she paid for it again, though she had a cancelled check for the same amount in hand. It must have been her mistake, she insisted, or *mine.* And even if it wasn't, she said she "didn't want to bother anybody at the travel agency or the credit card company" because "they must be too busy for this nonsense."

Of course, not all people act on their dominant emotional money association all of the time. Indeed, it is not uncommon for people to unwittingly pay an odd sort of homage to the "flip side" of their neurosis by engaging in behaviors that seem in direct opposition to it.

Many of us have come across scrimpers who tip opulently and spendthrifts who argue heatedly over a pittance. We've met someone who deems an insured money market account too risky but drops a week's pay in a slot machine, or an ultraorganized nickel-and-dime watcher who admits sheepishly that though he notes down every penny of outgo, he does not balance his checkbook. "They must be right," he insists. "After all, they're *the bank.*"

The money behavior of such people may take wild swings as their attitudes suddenly shift gears. An ex-roommate recalls:

> I used to share a Manhattan apartment with a woman who constantly threw money around. She bought her food in gourmet shops, ordered clothes from dozens of upscale catalogues every month, and thought nothing of dropping eighty dollars on a jar of night cream. I never saw her buy anything on sale either. She just bought what she wanted when she wanted it. Well, one December the New York City Transit Authority announced that the price of subway tokens was going up fifteen cents on the first of January. They also announced they were limiting token purchases to ten per customer until the new fare went into effect. Suddenly my roommate became obsessed. She spent days going from one subway station to another, buying ten tokens at every token booth. She started filling up jars with them and calculating just how much money she had saved and how many months she would be able to go without buying tokens at the new higher rate. It was strange, to say the least. Especially because she claimed to hate the subway and more often than not took cabs.

The preceding anecdotes are extreme cases, to be sure. Out at the edge of the money-madness spectrum. But their themes are far more prevalent than one might at first suppose. Even those who are not given to such extremes may well recognize echoes of attitudes they occasionally notice themselves experiencing and actions they occasionally undertake in an inexplicable "fit" of exaggerated and exacerbated money neurosis. Yet we must not be embarrassed about our financial "fits." Nor should we deny our propensity for them. We must instead acknowledge them, explore them, and attempt to understand them. For therein lies the key to cultivating more reasonable money attitudes.

Money will always and forever be part of the real world and part of our imagination. The trick for us all is to maneuver as thoughtfully and skillfully as our inconsistent psyches permit in the vast realm between the two. To sort out the real from the unreal, let us take a closer look at the many factors which contribute to the formation of the Money Complex.

THE FIVE-LAYERED MONEY COMPLEX

Though we come into the world with certain undeniable temperamental leanings, our basic personalities are to a large extent molded and modified by life experiences. They are influenced by the emotional dynamics of our earliest infancy, by our interactions with our families, by our friends, teachers, and neighbors, by our cultural and religious milieu, and in the modern world by technology and the constant hum of mass media. So, too, are our money personalities.

This book posits that each person's particular Money Complex consists of five successive layers which in general mirror the levels of human development. Its First Layer, the intrapsychic layer, stretches back as far as infancy, when emotional foundations are laid that will determine an individual's responses to situations far into the future. Its Second Layer, the family-training layer, begins soon after the First Layer, when children first become aware of money as a significant entity about which their parents have strong feelings (which they express verbally and nonverbally). Its Third Layer, the social-training layer, begins to form when children venture forth into the world and become the recipients of money messages conveyed in the classroom and outside it—at play, at the movies, at the shopping mall, at church, and so on.

It is usually in young adulthood that we begin to grapple with the Fourth Layer of the Complex, the layer that encompasses our emotional reactions to the techniques and technology of money and credit instruments. As we make our initial firsthand acquaintance with personal checking accounts, credit cards, and the like, we must learn to cope not just with tangible money we hold in our hands, but with a profusion of intangible representations and documentations. We must form attitudes about plastic cards and electronic blips and about the endless chores involved in processing countless pieces of financial paperwork.

When we are somewhat established in the world as adults, possess some capital, and wish to make our money multiply in the stock market or other financial markets, the Fifth—and final—Layer of the Complex, "pack-think," begins to have significant bearing on our money personalities. Even those of us who as autonomous individuals manage to behave rationally toward money most of the time may be prone to all manner of irrational actions when we fall prey to "pack-think" and get caught up in the throes of the mass fear and greed that motivate crowds of investors. For money represents more than just an individual reality. It represents, by its very nature, a powerful collective reality. The beliefs that any large group comes to jointly hold true about money or its equivalents help to define money in the minds of that group's members and to influence members' financial perspectives and perceptions.

Within any one person's psyche, different layers of the Money Complex are apt to provoke different thoughts and feelings about money. These thoughts and feelings create a chorus of internal voices that provoke attitudes and evoke particular behaviors. Sometimes one attitude wins out; sometimes another emerges as victor. Sometimes a compromise occurs in an attempt to quiet the maelstrom of conflict brewing beneath the surface of consciousness.

An internal money dialogue may go something like this:

SITUATION Mr. C. must make a decision as to whether or not to invest in an expensive new computer system for his graphic design business.

LAYER 1 (INTRAPSYCHIC) RESPONSE I hate to spend large sums of money. It goes against my grain. I don't know what it is, but I always feel ripped off after I write a large check, no matter what I get in return.

LAYER 2 (FAMILY-TRAINING-BASED) RESPONSE My parents always told me to err on the side of caution. They're probably right. I'd better stick with what I've got, or I'll end up in the poorhouse.

LAYER 3 (SOCIAL-TRAINING-BASED) RESPONSE On the other hand, all my heroes in business have gone out on a limb at one time or another. And I don't want my friends and colleagues in this field to think I can't keep up with them. Besides, all the ads for this new computer system are very appealing. They make me want to rush out and get one while they're still in stock.

LAYER 4 (TECHNOLOGY-BASED) RESPONSE Hey, maybe I could take out a loan or extend my line of credit. Maybe I could amortize the cost of the computer and take more tax deductions. Oh, but that's all too confusing. And if I call my accountant, he'll just talk gibberish and get me more confused. I'd rather just write a check and forget about it.

LAYER 5 (PACK-THINK) RESPONSE And gosh, this computer system must really be something. I heard that the manufacturer's stock went up ten points when it was introduced and another five points last quarter. You know, maybe if buying the system will save me money in the long run, like the salesman says it will, I can take *that* money and buy some stock in the company, too. A lot of my friends say it hasn't come close to peaking yet. Let's see, if it goes up five points every quarter for five years and I invest $10,000 . . . well, that's pretty complicated to figure, but it's a lot! Hmmm, what to do?

What *will* Mr. C. do? His character predisposes him to hold fast to his money and so do his internalized parental communications. Generally, those are extremely compelling unconscious voices, and if he heeds them he will not buy the new computer system. On the other hand, Mr. C. *also* seems particularly prone to capitulate to peer pressure and appears to be susceptible to advertising and marketing messages. He also appears to get swept up in the fervor of mass enthusiasms of the moment. If he heeds *these* voices, he will buy. In Mr. C.'s case, the techniques and technology of money and credit serve only to enhance his confusion. Because he panics at the complexities of loan payments and tax deductions, he tends to throw up his hands rather than do the appropriate calculations or consult effectively with people who will advise him based on their own calculations. His tendency to get swept up in "pack-think" fantasy scenarios of endless stock appreciation and pots of gold at the end of a rainbow serves to complicate matters as well.

Mr. C. seems to have weak spots at all layers of the Money Complex. He has a jumble of money messages in his mind and perhaps little awareness of where they come from. His resultant behavior could be hard to predict. But one thing seems certain: Whatever decision he makes—to buy or not to buy— will be profoundly emotional.

Fortunately, we need not be left in suspense over the outcome. In real life, Mr. C. did the following: He bought the computer system but felt miserable about his purchase, experiencing guilt, depression, and resentment in the aftermath of his action. He says he's still not certain whether the new system will ultimately save him money or not, but that he "really doesn't care," because every time he looks at the new computer, he "feels a burning hole in the pocket" and gets angry at the man who "talked him into it."

. . . .

In the following five chapters, the Five Layers of the Money Complex will be explored one at a time, from the bottom up. It is hoped that such an investigation will prove valuable to anyone who has ever been, at any time, a victim of money pathology. For it is through awareness that we may hope to be spared the tortures of Mr. C.

2

PART

- - - - - - - - -

The
Shape of the
Money
Complex

- - - - - - - - -

2

. . . .

Dirty Money
. . . and Other
Metaphors

. . . .

Every guinea is a philosopher's stone.

—LORD BYRON

THE TAG LINE of an ad campaign for a financial publication lamented the fact that "money doesn't come with instructions." Yet, by the time a child is old enough to begin conceptualizing money in practical terms, a foundation of unconscious instructions regarding the ways he will think and feel about it, as well as what he will do with it, has already been laid. He will be predisposed to respond to the stimulus of money in certain ways because many of his character traits and tendencies will already have been formed.

These character bents—and the emotional money associations that go along with them—constitute the first and often the most intractable layer of the Money Complex. Although they are by no means the only forces which determine our attitudes toward the comings and goings of money, they are, to be sure, potent ones. And where money-related behavior is most absurd, we may guess that it is at least in part influenced by roots that plunge deep, deep down into early experience, as in these instances:

Mr. D. owns a small public relations agency.
His employees find him difficult—some would say

impossible—to deal with. He refuses to hire an office manager and oversees all financial transactions himself, checking and rechecking his ledgers with great fastidiousness. Requests for petty cash above and beyond a subsistence-level weekly allocation, even when wholly justifiable, are often met with tirades of anger and indignation. As a result, any out-of-the-ordinary circumstance is bound to bring the office to a standstill. When a larger than usual mailing is required, for example, the postage meter setting stands at zero for days after it is done, halting service to other clients. When a piece of office equipment breaks down, Mr. D. is loath to spend the necessary money to fix it, and his secretary has been known to work on a portable typewriter she carries in from home while her boss stalls for weeks before deigning to let her call the repairman. The secretary describes Mr. D. as the most stubborn man she ever met.

Mrs. E. has an income level substantially lower than most of her neighbors. She and her husband bought their house in what became a relentlessly upscale neighborhood long before property values appreciated and people wealthier than themselves moved in. Yet, despite her lack of financial parity, Mrs. E., much to her husband's chagrin, joins whatever chic social clubs her new friends join, buys as many expensive new outfits as they do, and entertains by throwing the same kinds of costly dinners and cocktail parties. She says she would "rather die" than ever utter the simple phrase "I cannot afford it," and that she far prefers going into debt to ever "losing face" among the people who surround her. She quarrels repeatedly with her husband, imploring him to take a second job or ask for exorbitant raises in order that they may have more of what their neighbors have.

Ms. F. earns an enviable salary as an executive
television producer, yet she can never manage to put
any funds aside. Each paycheck is spent before she
cashes it, and she is continually worried that for
some reason or other the next check will not materialize. "Maybe the computers will make a mistake," she says, "and the check will be late. Or
maybe I'll be fired. It's such a crazy business." She
frets that she may have to call her parents for help
and wonders what will become of her if they will
not oblige. She envisions herself destitute and alone.
When her check does arrive on schedule on alternate Friday mornings, she experiences a sense of relief bordering on euphoria. She thinks, Ah, now I
feel like myself again. By Saturday afternoon she is
once again spending furiously at her favorite boutiques and department stores, depleting her resources and beginning the cycle of anxiety anew.

As we shall see, the money-related behaviors of these three
people have been ignited by attitudes informed by one of the
three most problematic—and most primal—emotional money
associations known to the mind of man. They spring from one
of three key money metaphors: money as filth; money as food;
and money as a security blanket.

Let us begin our investigation of these metaphors by elu-
cidating the first metaphor—the one that drives Mr. D. to do
what he does. It is a money metaphor that Sigmund Freud
began to shed light upon many years ago.

GARBAGE AND GOLD

Freud might well have appreciated a front-page story that appeared in the *Wall Street Journal* on November 28, 1988. Head-
lined "What Am I Bid on This Fine Sewage Filled with Gold?"
it recounted the plight of Igloo, South Dakota, a town which
had the misfortune to lie downwind of 300,000 tons of raw

sewage and sewage ash piled twenty feet high in giant sheds just west of the Black Hills.

The citizens of Igloo wound up in their unenviable predicament when a small Nebraska-based waste-control company, which had been hired to cart the refuse *out* of neighboring Minnesota, persuaded South Dakota to let them bring it *in*. The sewage contained gold, the waste-control company contended. Sixty million dollars' worth. They would use "gold reactor" technology to extract it, they vowed, creating three hundred jobs in the process.

Alas, the gold reactors never materialized. The doors of the warehouse that held the sewage were battered open by the Great Plains winds, and the foul stuff went everywhere, "rising up in odiferous brown dust devils at every breezy provocation."

South Dakota, which, after all, had to do something, declared it would put the sewage up for sale. Apparently it did contain an infinitesimal amount of gold, a tiny fraction of what the waste-control company had estimated. The state government reasoned that someone, somewhere might be tempted by this glittering lure.

Well, why not? *They* were tempted. Indeed, schemes to transmute base or common substances into gold—the ultimate, the rarest, the most mystical currency of all ("Whoever possesses it," said Christopher Columbus, "can even get souls into Paradise")—have captured the human imagination since the days when alchemists searched for the "philosopher's stone," which they believed would create gold from copper, lead, and iron.

Today we know, or say we know, that the alchemists wasted their time. Yet we still suspend disbelief where gold is at stake, falling prey in droves to "dirt-pile" scams in which promoters con credulous investors into buying gold that is still in the ground—not in a mine but, say, in a Southwestern desert—by promising that "revolutionary new processes" can extract the valuable ore. According to the North American Securities Administration Association, investors spend about a quarter of a billion dollars a year literally buying dirt.

No doubt Freud would have been intrigued by dirt-pile stories too. For they, like the South Dakota debacle, serve to illustrate the fundamental concept he contributed to the psychology of money.

To the unconscious mind, Freud said, money *equals* dirt. More precisely, it equals the basest sort of filth imaginable—excrement.

In his patients' dreams and free associations, as well as in myths, fairy tales, and folklore, Freud found evidence that supported the money-excrement connection. Even as far back as ancient Babylonian times, he noted, gold was referred to as "the feces of hell."

In a paper called "Character and Anal Eroticism," Freud hypothesized that the specific identification between "the most precious substance known to man and the most worthless, which they reject as waste matter," stemmed from the very contrast implied. We tend to experience reality in terms of pairs of opposites—day and night, black and white, good and evil—and so we have an unconscious bent for linking these opposites and displacing our feelings from one psychic pole to another. What we love we hate. What we value we devalue. What is worth much seems also, somehow, to be worthless.

We do not have to resort to deciphering Babylonian texts to find for ourselves corroboration of Freud's infamous equation. We can find it in our own vernacular, in which one becomes "stinking rich" upon making a "pot" of "filthy lucre" (which, if it's made illegally, has to be "laundered"). We can find it in the words of Shakespeare, in whose *Othello* we read, "He who steals my purse steals trash." We can find it in the lyrics of rock star Don Henley, who tells us, "If dirt were dollars, we'd all be in the black."

If we have any residual doubt about how deeply we connect money and filth, we need only observe how far some of our more prestigious institutions go in an attempt to sublimate and deny the connection. In what are known as better banks, customers receive only clean new bills in transactions with tellers. In certain private clubs, such as San Francisco's Pacific Union Club, coins brought in by members are scoured and buffed before the waiters offer them as change—on little silver trays.

Why would so many people go to such lengths to spruce up and sanitize something if they did not perceive it as fundamentally unclean?

There's a well-known tenet of economics called Gresham's Law. Named for its originator, who served in the sixteenth century as Queen Elizabeth's Master of the Mint, it states that bad money drives out good money. When two metals, say gold and silver, are in circulation, the cheaper (silver) becomes the more prevalent medium of exchange, while the more expensive (gold) is hoarded or melted down.

Gresham's Law makes perfect economic sense. The more expensive currency will only appreciate in value as it becomes increasingly difficult to obtain. Yet Gresham's Law makes a kind of metaphorical sense as well.

We would like to think of our money as *good* money, *worthy* money, *clean* money. Yet in our unconscious mind the symbolic idea of *tainted* money, *dirty* money, *bad* money keeps nudging the good aside. Like the proverbial bad penny, it just keeps on turning up.

But how does this universal unconscious link affect our individual behavior toward money? Freud had an answer for that as well.

Taking his theory a step further, he hypothesized that our collective association of excrement and money becomes personalized, i.e., appropriated for the individual unconscious and thus for personal neurosis, during the period of toilet training.

In the second and third years of life the child is for the first time asked to "produce" something of "value" so that his parents might be proud of him. It is also during this time span that children come to experience some degree of autonomy. They realize that they can convert their actions, or non-actions, into intentions that impact on their environment and on those with whom they interact. Suddenly they are aware that they possess a degree of influence and control.

Freud theorizes that the dynamics, demands, and frustrations of toilet training as carried out within each family are registered within each child's psyche, and that the ways in which the child chooses to set limits, or not, and exert his power, or not, are later transferred into the financial realm. The first body product is so significant, he postulated, that even when preoccupation with it is extinguished, conflicts and conundrums surrounding it are later inevitably projected onto a "grown-up" object of equal significance: money.

Following this theory to its logical conclusion, the idea is that children who revel in praise over their successful "deposits," coming to regard them as gifts to their beloved parents, to whom they feel indebted, may grow up to spend without undue hesitation or reluctance. Conversely, those who refuse to empty their bowels in childhood, except when they absolutely must, may refuse to readily empty their pockets as adults.

Freud's monetary writings focused heavily on this latter dynamic. He observed patients suffering from financial "constipation," as it were, and by tracing their early history, concluded that the pleasure they gained in holding on to their first "savings"—a pleasure so intense he referred to it as a facet of *anal eroticism*—was a sensation they were able to re-experience later on by becoming overly economical. They achieved satisfaction from hoarding their precious possessions, and they chose to hold on even in the face of other needs, often more rational and more pressing needs.

To this sort of person Freud gave the name "anal character." And he observed that the anal character displays a cluster of three distinct personality traits: orderliness, obstinacy, and parsimony.

ANALITY IN ACTION

The concept of the anal character, through the work of Freud and some of his followers (notably Karl Abraham, who in a well-known essay on the topic cited a famous case of "an eccentric miser who used to go about his house with the front of his trousers unbuttoned in order that the buttonholes should not wear out too quickly"), has achieved popularization. It's become quite common to hear someone described as being "anal," and we all seem to more or less understand what is implied when the term is used.

Nearly all of us seem to have at least one quintessentially anal character in our life. He is the person who wants to know, as he painstakingly scrutinizes the restaurant check at the culmination of a dinner for twelve, just who ordered the second moo shu pork. He is the one who will call the operator from a pay phone, despite the growing line of people waiting behind him, to report a lost quarter and offer his mailing address for a refund check. He is the diehard coupon clipper and penny-pincher, the one who would rather suffer the tortures of the damned than even consider tossing out a sheaf of papers with the paper clip still attached.

Indeed, just as Freud noted, running parallel to his tight-fistedness, we often find in the anal character traits of excessive tidiness and stubbornness. More often than not, his sock drawer is a paragon of organization and his desktop a study in right angles. His recipes are indexed and his photographs catalogued. If he ever goes to bed without flossing his teeth, it's probably because he's running a fever of 104. He may feel uncomfortable leaving the house unless all the money in his wallet is facing in the same direction and arranged by graduating denominations. And if you even hint that he might wish to relax his habits, he will firmly set his jaw, fold his arms across his chest, and blink at you as if you had suddenly sprouted a second head.

The financial behaviors of anal characters seem to have very little to do with how much money they actually possess. Anyone's emotional development can steer them in this direction. Even those with a surplus of money can feel compelled to hang on to it beyond all reason.

Reading the life history of Wallis Simpson, who was to become the Duchess of Windsor, might lead one to conclude she was a virtual textbook example of the anality principle.

Despite the substantial dowry with which her abdicated monarch came endowed, she paid scrupulous attention to financial detail. Her household staff was required to submit bills itemized down to the last cent in order to validate expenses. She reportedly haggled constantly over plumbers' and electricians' bills. She was known to patrol her house relentlessly, checking that the lights in broom closets had been switched off.

The Duchess most assuredly fit the rest of the overall character profile that Freud sketched out as well. A veritable demon for order, she would, biographer Charles Higham writes, "move a chair a fraction of an inch if its position had been changed by a cleaning woman." She insisted that her bed linen be ironed every night and replaced every other night, and that the lettuce leaves for her salad be trimmed to the same shape and size before being served.

Just as the Duchess offers an exemplary illustration of anality in action, so does our own Mr. D. Mr. D., you will recall, is the perennially penny-pinching boss so loath to part with money he let essential office equipment go unrepaired.

Were we to take a stab at understanding Mr. D.'s money attitude based on early character development, we might guess that this is a man who did not at age two readily comply with his parents' demands. Today he's *still* trying to do things his way. No matter how many people pressure him to take action to the contrary, his character is such that he cannot bear to part with money even when he knows on an objective level that doing so will be to his benefit.

Clearly, anal characters can annoy the living daylights out of those who come into contact with them. The more precisely they conform to the textbook profile, the more infuriating they can be. Even far less pronounced cases than the Duchess can drive friends, relatives, and colleagues to distraction.

But it is worth keeping in mind that a bent toward anality, while offering those who possess it the satisfaction of retention and the pleasure of control, nevertheless brings them displeasure as well. Parting with money they do not wish to part with—as inevitably they must sometimes do—often brings on keen feelings of misery. Thus they deprive themselves of the joys of even the most minor self-indulgences, not to mention the emotional rewards of giving and sharing.

What's more, those with anal attitudes may only perceive money as "precious" when it's being held on to. They may perceive it instead as shameful, even "disgusting," when it's on the loose. Consequently, while they may dedicate themselves to hanging on to what resources they've got, they may unconsciously arrange not to attract much more money. As to the concept of risking a bit of money to reap a good deal more down the line—well, that may prove abhorrent to them.

It is also worth noting, however, that even the most resolutely anal character tends to harbor within himself impulses toward contrary behavior. Whether those impulses get acted out in small ways, such as carelessly paying an electric bill twice, or in major sprees, as when the Duchess and a girlfriend waltzed into a fine linen store and in a flash spent $25,000 on elegant bedding, one can generally spot vivid flickers of opposition to an overriding "tight" characterological bent.

A number of therapists who followed Freud agreed that his prevalent money theory, i.e., the anality theory, was "true" so far as their clinical experience bore out, but was only a part of the truth about the Money Complex. While it serves to explain quite handily the retentive aspects of money psychology, it does little to enlighten us about the desire to acquire. That desire is, it appears, tied to another unconscious money metaphor. As psychoanalyst Otto Fenichel pointed out in a paper called "The Drive to Amass Wealth," money can represent anything that can be given or taken, including mother's milk.

Freud himself briefly studied this phenomenon. In *The Psychopathology of Everyday Life*, published seven years before "Character and Anal Eroticism," Freud noted, "Among the majority even of what are called 'respectable people' traces of divided behavior can easily be observed where money and propriety are concerned." His musings on money in that particular passage concluded with this observation: "It may perhaps be generally true that the primitive greed of the suckling, who wants to take possession of every object (in order to put it in his mouth), has only been incompletely overcome by civilization and upbringing."

So, though Freud seemed to drop the ball on this one down the line, we may infer that at this stage of his career he was at least toying with the notion that attitudes toward money may also be shaped in the oral phase, a period of infancy that occurs even before we are two or three years of age.

MONEY HUNGRY

As infants, we have only an internal reality. We have nary a clue where we end and the outside world begins. Our impulses drive us to try and incorporate that world by taking it in as food. Later, this drive to ingest the objects that surround us will be sublimated into a drive to acquire money.

Once again, if we but look to language, the connection between symbol and substance—in this case between food and money—becomes evident. In slang, money can be "bread," "dough," "lettuce," and "clams"—even "gravy" and "sugar"—just to name a few of its culinary sobriquets.

On an emotional level, we can't fail to notice the connection as well. People who have had grandparents or a doting favorite aunt press twenty-dollar bills on them as urgently as they press that third helping of pasta, pot roast, potato kugel, or pecan pie will recognize the similarities instantly. ("Here, here, take it, take it! You need it! If you don't, my feelings will be hurt!")

On the popular TV situation comedy "Family Ties," Alex Keaton's mother, Elise, once told a story about when her lucre-loving son was small and she had to take him to the hospital because he "swallowed a dollar." "You are what you eat," Alex quipped in response. As children, many of us literally tried eating money. Our parents attempted to stop us from swallowing actual pennies and dimes, but they also offered us as a special treat coins of chocolate wrapped in elaborate golden foil.

Upscale versions of symbolic money eating persist well beyond the parameters of childhood. At a 1988 six-course luncheon where then-presidents-elect George Bush and Carlos Salinas de Gortari of Mexico were feted by Houston's power elite, dessert consisted of chocolate truffles coated with edible eighteen-karat gold (these delicacies presented an interesting problem when they kept setting off the security metal detectors). In the mid-1980s go-go days at the firm of Salomon Brothers, traders didn't exactly eat money, but they ritually performed what Michael Lewis, author of *Liar's Poker*, terms "astonishing feats of gluttony" while making it. Beginning with a round of onion cheeseburgers at 8 A.M., increasingly corpulent wheelers and dealers would make "enormous cartons of malted milk balls disappear in two gulps" and order guacamole "in five-gallon drums."

Most of us, at least figuratively speaking, have an appetite for money. But when someone is compulsive about money acquisition, i.e., "money-hungry," we often call him piggish. There is, in fact, a Wall Street adage that goes "There's room for the bears and room for the bulls. There's no room for the pigs."

Poor misunderstood pigs, however, have earned a bum rap in this regard. Despite their gluttonous reputation, pigs actually back away from their troughs when they've eaten an adequate amount of food.* When it comes to orality, pigs know instinctively when enough is enough. Unfortunately, many of us humans do not.

British psychoanalyst Melanie Klein wrote extensively about the infant's relationship to his mother's breast and the

---

* Scientists have discovered that pigs actually have an internal "stop eating" button in the form of a hormone known as CCK, which prevents them from gorging. The hormone is a cause of much chagrin to pork producers who want their hogs to be fatter so they in turn can sell more paté and earn more money.

nourishment that comes from it. She points out that in the oral phase of development, roughly the first twelve to eighteen months of life, babies alternate between feelings of gratification, which occur when they are feeding or full, and feelings of frustration, which occur when they are hungry.

Along with satiation, Klein says, come feelings of gratitude and also feelings of generosity. Feelings of deprivation, on the other hand, lead to envy (someone else has what I want), jealousy (someone else has what I want *from whom I want it*), and greed (though I have what you might think is enough, I want more).

The oral stage has also come to be known as the stage of *primary narcissism.* During its first year, the utterly self-involved infant wants not only to be fed with actual food but with actions which are symbolically related to food and which yield emotional succor. Caresses, cuddles, cooing, and the mother's mirroring and echoing actions—facial expressions and gestures through which the mother nonverbally reassures the baby that he is loved and understood and valued for himself—all serve to "fill up" the infant.

Naturally, since continual feeding and holding of the infant is out of the question, all babies will experience doses of both gratification and frustration as they develop. "The infant's longing for an inexhaustible and always present breast," Klein wrote, "can never fully be satisfied."

A degree of frustration should not cause excessive later life problems, provided that parental care, though not perfect, was good enough, which is to say provided that the parents offered an adequate supply of actual nourishment in the form of food and emotional nourishment in the form of empathy and positive attention. But traumas during this period, in the form of imbalances between satiation and unsatisfied longing, can have dramatic implications for one's psychological health. They seem clearly to have implications for one's financial health as well.

Overly frustrated infants may grow into adults who have a low tolerance for failure, who feel worthless, who abhor criticism, and who require constant bolstering and adulation. In the society we have created, many of the good feelings and narcissistic "supplies" such individuals crave can be purchased with the coin of the realm. By getting and spending, they can convey an image of themselves that they don't believe they can live up to in reality. The more money they acquire, the greater their opportunity to hide behind this image.

In our world, we can buy a car that says, "I'm important." We can buy a house, put in a pool, and announce, "I am worthier than my neighbor, who must drive to the beach in order to swim." We can fill up our closets and our jewelry cases and our breakfronts with objects that fill up our own emptiness. It is a temptation difficult to resist if we do not feel good about ourselves. (It is not shocking that Imelda Marcos, world champion shoe shopper, was heard to lament, "I come from a third-rate province in a Third World country.") For we are wont to believe that money not only fills us up but fills us out, that, as the old tongue-in-cheek Yiddish proverb asserts, "With money in your pocket, you are wise and you are handsome and you sing well, too."

The only problem is that using getting-and-spending as a means of gaining self-esteem never works for long.

If we were to speculate on the early history of our Mrs. E.—the "poor neighbor" whose drive to amass money and its equivalents can only be described as frantic—we might guess that her infantile longings for nourishment, literal or psychical, were not adequately sated. She never formed an image of herself as a being of value and having integrity. Now she must make sure she gets what others have in order to prove her worthiness—to her neighbors, yes, but also to herself—whatever the cost.

Yes, her acquisitions bring her gratification—for a time. But any compulsive spender knows deep down that a hole in the heart is never filled for long by a Porsche or a Montblanc pen. Always there is a nagging re-emerging space that must be stuffed and padded and packed. If we keep on filling the space with additional money or money equivalents, we can never tackle its root cause.

Nevertheless, many people try and try again to satiate their "hunger" by getting and spending, just as many of them attempt to pleasure and fortify themselves by hoarding what small or large sums of money they've already got. Oral and anal implications for the psychopathology of money seem indisputable. Yet there is still another infantile stage that has financial ramifications.

SECURITY BLANKETS AND TEDDY BEARS

Between the initial oral phase of life when we wish to incorporate the world, and the anal phase when we begin to register the reality of our separateness, between the time of taking in and the time of being asked to *give* in lies an in-between realm that pediatrician and psychoanalyst D. W. Winnicott named the *transitional phase.* It is a time of identity confusion and anxiety when, as psychiatrist and author Robert Coles has so nicely put it, we move from an attitude of an all-embracing "Yes!" to one of a stubborn "No, No!" via a period of "Oh! Oh!"

In such a phase we make use of what Winnicott termed *transitional objects,* which have more popularly become known as *comfort objects.* We become deeply attached to a particular blanket, handkerchief, doll, or teddy bear that we perceive all at once as being inside us, outside us, and at the border where we intersect with the world. What exactly the object *is* is of far less importance than the nature of our relationship to it.

Most parents who have observed their children's relationships to comfort objects inherently understand a few things about them and observe certain rules for the objects' care. Because the child has developed an intense reliance on the object—not unreminiscent of the child's reliance on the parents themselves—the parents know it must be packed when taking the child on an outing. It has become a psychic necessity, and if it's not taken along a miserable time will be guaranteed for all. With the comfort object nearby, the baby will engage in a kind of self-hypnosis. He will gurgle, sing, smile, and often have the good grace to fall asleep at bedtime. Without it, he becomes anxious and forlorn, eager to apprise the entire household of his woe.

The parents also tacitly agree to allow the object to grow shabby and to never repair it. When the baby tatters and batters it, he's expressing not only a deep loving attachment but also an aggressive force. He mutilates it—and thus endows it with meaning—because he loves it and hates it.

Lastly, the parents allow the object to grow redolent with the smells of the baby and do not launder it as often as they might deem ideal. When it is cleaned, the baby becomes distraught, for then it is no longer special. The quality of specialness that has been lost is nothing less than a quality of "selfhood." If the toy or doll no longer smells like the baby, the child is no longer reassured by the idea that it feels like a part of him.

Though most of us may not remember our own particular transitional objects, our parents might well recall just what it was we cherished so ardently. At the very least, they will probably remember that somewhere along the line we had *something* that made us feel better, especially when they were not around to cling to. Those with children of their own, of course, can watch the process happening all over again.

If each of us went through a period where we became deeply reliant on an object that we perceived as necessary for secure survival, if our very sense of identity became wrapped up in the object, and if we used it to act out our deep-seated ambivalence, it stands to reason that such a crucial object would be less likely to disappear entirely from the psychic realm than it would be—as excrement and mother's milk are—to get transformed into something else.

We may put our blankets and teddy bears behind us, and

they themselves may lose all meaning, yet we reconstruct emotions and behaviors we had in connection with them when we deal with cash, credit, and coin. For, in many significant respects, money is perfectly suited to serve as an adult psychic security blanket.

Some of us use money as a self-soothing agent. We may perceive it as a hedge against anxiety and uncertainty, as compensation for various kinds of loss, and as a deterrent, if only a temporary one, to feelings of loneliness, sadness, and despair. ("Money cures melancholy," goes a British proverb.)

Many of us have a love-hate relationship with money, which we act out in endless repeating scenarios wherein we can't seem to decide whether or not we really want it. (Money and ambivalence were made for each other. We feel ambivalently toward things which we perceive as finite, yet needed— and money certainly fits that bill.)

Lastly, to some degree, we invest money with a symbolic quality of "selfhood." As with our security blankets of yore, we perceive money as being linked with personal identity.

Much evidence exists to substantiate the psychic link between money and self. Indeed, the fantasy of literally seeing oneself reflected in money has been verbally expressed by children early on. When a cereal company surveyed children aged five to ten as to whose face they would most like to see on the dollar bill, the most prevalent answer was "Mine." (Abraham Lincoln ran a poor second.) And even in adult life the temptation to affix an image of oneself onto money may prove irresistible. According to *New York* magazine, *USA Today* founder and Gannett chairman Al Neuharth offered his retirement luncheon guests a memento of his reign in the form of brass coins bearing his image—along with little rosewood cases in which to display them.

Throughout history, humankind has emblazoned its coins and imprinted its paper tender with portraits of the rulers, gods, and totem animals that we follow and revere, and with whom we therefore associate ourselves. We have adorned money as well with images and slogans that express our prevalent philosophical and religious ideas, our political loyalties, and our cultural mythology—in short, with images that define our values and ideals. (On the back of a one-dollar bill, for example, one finds a veritable cornucopia of democratic American values displayed on the Great Seal of the United States.) The dynamic can work in reverse as well. When an idea or a ruling figure is no longer viable or credible—and when we no longer wish to identify ourselves with it but to disassociate ourselves from it—it may hastily disappear from the face of currency, as when coins bearing the image of the cruel despot Caligula were called in and melted down after his death.

Just as we make tangible connections between ourselves and our money, we make intangible emotional connections. To a certain extent, when most of us look into the mirror we see money gazing back. We think to ourselves, I make this much. I owe that much. I have this much. By the time I'm X years older, I should have that much more. Assessing our financial "position" is part of the way we describe ourselves to ourselves.

In and of itself, as we shall see in later chapters, this entanglement of personal identity and money can create some knotty problems. But when in a single personality it is especially pronounced, and when it intermingles in that same personality with attitudes of extreme anxiety and ambivalence toward money, what we get is someone like Ms. F., the subject of the third case history at the start of this chapter. Ms. F., you will recall, is the television producer who tormented herself with thoughts of impending pennilessness.

One may suspect that whatever early experiences Ms. F. endured in infancy, they brought her little sense of security, stability, or constancy. She apparently still needs something to cling to in the face of her fragmented feelings, and her psyche has designated money as that "something."

For Ms. F., money has—to a very exaggerated degree—taken on all the properties of a transitional object or security blanket. When she has money in her hand, she is ecstatic and all seems right with the world. When the money is gone, she is nervous and bereft. She loses track of her equilibrium and of her center, of her very feeling that the world makes sense. She imagines that only her parents will be able to save her from such feelings, but simultaneously fears they won't oblige.

She employs money as a kind of emotional glue that holds her together. Yet, in spite of all this, she repeatedly arranges for money to disappear shortly after it appears. Like Mr. D. and Mrs. E., her behavior is redundant. Like them, she does not seem able to benefit from the lessons of experience, and opts instead to repeat and repeat.

THE POWER OF METAPHOR

Repetition is perhaps the biggest clue that the money attitudes of all three of these people are grounded in large part in the First Layer of the Money Complex. Their actions seem to emanate from some sort of predetermined script, and the people perpetrating the actions seem unable, almost unauthorized, to alter their roles through spontaneity or improvisation.

Each of our three subjects seems to have experienced some "glitch" in the course of early development—which never runs smoothly. That's why we don't enter adulthood as paragons of adjustment to reality—that's why we are at least a wee bit neurotic in at least a few areas. But where these glitches are particularly severe, they will often attach themselves to money—that blank projection screen—in particularly neurotic fashions. The greater the traumas one incurs in infancy, the greater the likelihood that money will be misused as an expression of those traumas.

Why the repetition? Because primal metaphors in the psyche are not remembered in words and coherent images. Rather, the scenarios that led to their creation tend to get re-enacted. Though we do not consciously recall our infantile conflicts with regard to our mother's care and feeding, our toilet training, or our comfort objects, we live them out in behavioral patterns.

Why do we act them out? Because by doing so, we are unwittingly trying to correct and master any problems we originally had with regard to them. We want things to turn out differently than they did the first time—but, alas, as the consequences of the behaviors of Mr. D., Mrs. E., and Ms. F. indicate, they often do not.

The "sense" of money metaphors is a regressive kind of sense. Actions on behalf of those metaphors are consistent with archaic emotions that existed long before we could even speak. They hark back to a time when words signified nothing and feelings signified all. Though they did not stem from language, and though in fact they predated it, they have the power to influence language and even override it.

And that is one of the many reasons why it is so difficult to do one of the things we *should* do about money: Communicate rationally about it.

The next chapter will deal with the subject of money communications within the family. It will deal with the Second Layer of the Money Complex, the layer that is passed like a baton from one generation to the next.

3

. . . .

Moneygrams

. . . .

The dollar always talks in the end.

—DONALD TRUMP

WE ALREADY KNOW that an individual's money personality consists partly of a pleasure-seeking, frustration-avoiding id, partly of a rational ego, and partly of an overseeing conscience or superego. The primitive emotions we experience as infants and transform into money metaphors are based in the id. They occur before we are aware of actual money and its practical functions. But we are still quite young and impressionable when we begin to grow acquainted with the existence and practical uses of money in everyday life. At about that time, the monetary superego begins to gain a foothold in our psyches, forming the Second Layer of the Money Complex.

As toddlers beginning to be up and about in the world, our earliest perceptions of actual money are imbued with magical notions. We notice that something exists in the pockets of our parents (pockets we typically envision as eternally full), which, when extracted and presented to strangers, is instantly converted into anything that's wanted! A ride on the bus or a Ferris wheel. A hot dog or an ice cream cone. An entrance ticket to the baseball game or the zoo or even (though, hey, who really cares) brand-new socks and underwear.

Yet, before we know it, our money honeymoon is over. Hope becomes mingled with disenchantment as we begin to perceive that this amazing instrument can be a source of frustration as well as satisfaction.

In *The Moral Life of Children*, Robert Coles describes the

development of the superego as "months and months, years and years, of lessons learned, disappointments severely felt, difficulties endured and not forgotten." When it comes to learning about the true nature of money, difficulties and disappointments abound, and that is one of our earliest lessons of all.

Inevitably, it dawns on our developing minds that all kinds of "shoulds" and "shouldn'ts" are attached to money. We shouldn't ask questions about it. We shouldn't brag about it. We shouldn't spend the twenty-five dollars Grandma gave us for Christmas, because it has to go into something called a "college fund." We should count our pennies, because "a penny saved is a penny earned." We should put aside our money for a "rainy day" because it "doesn't grow on trees."

Typically, many of these "shoulds" and "shouldn'ts" emanate directly from our parents. Because we both admire and fear our mothers and our fathers, the instructions they impart to us hold great significance. By incorporating their dictums into our own minds, we do the next best thing to taking in our parents themselves.

Children harbor a desire to merge with parental figures. Experiments measuring subliminal perception have actually demonstrated the extent of this yearning. When the message "Mommy and I are one" is flashed across a screen so quickly that viewers cannot consciously register it, they nevertheless report feelings of health, strength, and optimism.

Of course, we cannot fully merge with our mothers and fathers psychically, in spite of our relentless oral strivings toward symbiotic oneness, and, in spite of our Oedipal longings, we cannot possess them physically. Yet we can and do hold on to them by carrying them around in our psyches, allotting them a permanent corner from which they more or less continually express their approval or their condemnation. Thus, the voices of our mothers and fathers, which loom large and loud throughout the many years of childhood, become an integral part of our adult faculty of self-judgment. We will forever appraise ourselves to a certain degree in terms of whether or not we're doing what they would want us to do.

But when it comes to money, what do they really want? How do we know?

WILLY LOMAN, KING LEAR, AND WALTER YOUNGER

In recent years, family therapists have begun studying something called *genograms*. Genograms are essentially graphic representations of emotional family trees. Whereas a genealogist might diagram a historical family tree to trace one's blood connections and heritage, a family therapist would construct a genogram to try and elucidate a different sort of legacy—the patterns of feelings and interaction that parents transmit to their daughters, sons, and grandchildren.

By looking back across two, three, or more generations, with an eye to which members of the family were emotionally close or distant, and to which family members might have been, say, addictive personalities, co-dependents, or suicidal personalities, insight can often be gained as to why an individual has a particular emotional problem or a particular set of conflicts that plagues him. Mood disorders, a propensity for temper tantrums or depression, for example, can be a kind of ongoing emotionally contagious theme in certain families as a result of learned behavior patterns. Money disorders, with their strong emotional components, can be contagious as well. If we want to understand our own Money Complex, we might think back over our family history and construct a kind of "moneygram" as a guide. For the way our money attitudes are formed and malformed has much to do with the way our families, knowingly or unknowingly, trained us.

That the uses and misuses of money play a powerful role in family dynamics has certainly not been lost on our best playwrights, who are themselves among the most astute students of human nature. To watch a production of Shakespeare's *King Lear*, Arthur Miller's *Death of a Salesman*, or Lorraine Hansberry's *A Raisin in the Sun* is to watch the drama of family money pathology unfold in front of our eyes, act by act, scene by scene.

Had any of us grown up with the vain, impetuous, and manipulative King Lear for a father, we might well have gotten the message, as his daughters Goneril and Regan did, that riches can be gained through excessive, albeit insincere, flattery and adulation. Butter up your father and half a kingdom shall be yours, read the royal family's script. And we might well have understood, as the unfortunate disinherited Cordelia came to understand, that honest affection and loyalty, unembellished with hyperbole and false praise, were not—at least not until it was too late—considered worthy of fiscal reward. ("Thy truth then be thy dower," Lear tells his youngest child when she declines to stroke his royal ego as her siblings have.)

Had we grown up with Arthur Miller's Willy Loman, we might well have learned, along with his confused and misguided sons, Happy and Biff, to view everyone in terms of how much money they earned ("When he walks into the store," Happy says of an acquaintance, "the waves part in front of him. That's fifty-two thousand dollars a year coming through that door"); to equate the obtaining of money and success with violence ("I decapitated them," Willy replies when a neighbor inquires about the success of his recent out-of-town business trip); to loathe ourselves for not living up to our grandiose financial expectations ("I'm a dime a dozen, Pop," says Biff, "and so are you"); to suffer chronic debilitating envy of anyone with a relatively secure financial life; and to concentrate on outbragging and outdreaming everyone else in the household, even as petty expenses mount up into a huge unmanageable heap of debt.

And had we grown up, as Lorraine Hansberry's Travis Younger did, in a poor trigenerational household practically torn apart by the infusion of a significant sum of money (a $10,000 death benefit from the boy's grandfather's life insurance policy, much of which is lost by Travis's father, Walter, in an ill-advised business scheme), we might have been overwhelmed by the degree to which a change in economic status, even one ostensibly for the better, can turn a family inside out, fuel the most bitter of quarrels, incite the most foolish behavior, and create an atmosphere of despair. (Though at the end of *A Raisin in the Sun*, it must be noted, Walter redeems himself from money madness.) Certainly one need not frequent the theater to see family money dynamics in action. We need only consider our own families with an eye to the money messages given and received to assure ourselves that the way we operate financially stems not only from the personal realm but from the interpersonal realm as well.

MONEY TALKS

Like all transgenerational messages, money messages come in several "flavors." Some are overt, some are covert, and some are deeply paradoxical, inconsistent, and confusing.

In many families, the prevailing money message is actually a metamessage. It goes: "We don't discuss money, and we don't discuss the fact that we don't discuss it."

Ever since Ralph Waldo Emerson wrote that "money is hardly spoken of in parlors without an apology," numerous reasons have been offered for the absence of meaningful personal money talk:

It has been suggested that rich people eschew discussing their money lest the poor figure out how to get some for themselves. Since we all take our cues as to proper social behavior from the upper economic echelons, as Thorstein Veblen pointed out in *The Theory of the Leisure Class*, it would follow that any behavior disdained by them would be disdained by many others in the name of "etiquette."

It has also been noted that superstition plays a role in our aversion. To talk of one's money, many believe, is to tempt the gods to snatch it away, to bring on the evil eye (*mal occhio*, as Italians might say, or a *kina hora*, as Eastern European Jews might call it).

But to the two reasons for such a widespread aversion, we must surely add the following:

Since we associate money with food, avoiding the subject can make us feel we appear less hungry, less needy, less greedy, and less vulnerable.

Since we associate it with filth, shunning discussion of it can be a way of fending off feelings of shame.

Since we associate money with self, speaking of our money can make us feel awkward and self-conscious. On some level we all seem to understand that revealing the way we feel about money reveals much about ourselves and the true story of our lives.

Given all this, it's no surprise that many of us try to avoid meaningful money discussions as assiduously as possible, even—or especially—among those who know us best, our own family members. Yet money messages, verbalized or not, are an inextricable component of family life. No child can help but be aware of his parents' money attitudes.

When parents give their children nonverbal communications which instruct them *not to communicate verbally*, it can often lead to trouble. For when children observe that a subject is treated with conspiratorial secrecy, they tend to become fascinated by it. The greater the degree of clandestineness and the deeper the family taboo, the greater the level of fascination. Unfortunately, the greater the fascination, the more potentially damaging fantasies are liable to grow. For where hard facts are unavailable, the imagination is only too happy to fill in the blanks.

A child whose questions about money go unanswered, or who notices his parents repeatedly steering their conversations away from money, or discussing it only in hushed tones and in arguments half heard from behind closed doors, may well come to associate money with unhappiness and strife. He may perceive it as something to be feared, or as something to feel guilty about. He may grow up imagining that his family is hiding money from him or, conversely, concealing the fact that they are hovering on the brink of ruin. He may also grow up to be money-phobic, turning into an adult who is all too willing to reject financial responsibility of any kind, protesting that he is incapable of understanding money and therefore wishes to have nothing to do with it.

Given how crippling family money-talk aversion can be, one might think that straightforward, clearly verbalized money messages imparted to a child are the key to fostering sensible, realistic financial attitudes. Indeed, sometimes they can be.

I once witnessed a father instructing his twelve-year-old daughter on the concept of debt and interest payments in a way she will doubtless recall. Intent upon purchasing several souvenirs at Washington, D.C.'s Air and Space Museum, to which the family had made a long-planned holiday excursion, the girl had apparently run rapidly through both her usual weekly allowance and the extra few dollars with which her parents had provided her to buy souvenirs. When she asked her father for more money, he agreed to give it to her, provided she understood that the additional cash was a loan.

When the girl asked, "What's a loan?" he took a blank sheet of paper and improvised an impromptu instruction. Ripping the sheet in half and offering it to her, he said, "Imagine I am giving you this much money, but I want you to give it back within a certain period of time." "Okay, sure," said his daughter, thinking, no doubt, that this loan stuff was a piece of cake. "Now," he added, tearing off another small corner of the paper,

"I'll want you to also give me back a little more than I gave you—because when you take a loan you owe something called 'interest.' "

The daughter no longer looked entirely delighted by the prospect of a loan, but the father assured her that the payment of reasonable interest was fair and, what's more, unavoidable when one borrowed in the real world. Together they decided the girl would borrow five dollars and together they worked out an interest rate (5 percent, since she was family after all) and a repayment schedule. At the end of the negotiation, both parties seemed satisfied. The girl had gotten what she wanted, with some tolerable strings attached; the father had successfully proffered what he considered to be an invaluable life lesson.

Would that things could always go so smoothly.

This, after all, was a lesson grounded in reality. The payment of interest is a financial fact of life. It was also a lesson offered calmly, with patience and affection.

Alas, other kinds of clearly articulated messages can have detrimental effects. Where lessons given are themselves a product of parental money neurosis, and where they are offered without rationale or without a caring affect behind them, they will reverberate in children's minds, all right, but in ways that can do more harm than good.

Karl Abraham, in his writings on money pathology, cited the case of a rich banker "who again and again impressed on his children that they should retain the contents of the bowels as long as possible, in order to get the benefit of every bit of expensive food they ate." If it seems downright frightening to contemplate how this gentleman's children may have turned out, it is even more disconcerting to realize that the number of people who receive comparably bizarre parental money messages seems to be nothing short of legion.

- My mother said only poor people went to heaven.
- My father said only criminals were wealthy.

- My parents warned me not to let anyone know we had money or they would jinx us.

- My parents said I was a popular kid because they were rich enough to have a house with a tennis court. They told me, quite plainly, that if one was without money, one would be without friends.

- My parents told me I had to grow up to be a success, or, being financially unsuccessful themselves, they would end up "charity cases."

- My mother always said a smart woman doesn't ever let a man know she's capable of making money.

- My father always said a man should never let a woman know he has money or she'll find a way to take it away from him.

- My parents said there was a "secret" to making money, but that no one in our family knew what it was. Making lots of money was something of which only "other people" were capable.

- My parents, who were quite well off, never let me spend a dime without my begging and pleading. They said I must never forget that we could "wake up poor in the morning." Sometimes I would lie awake at bedtime, afraid to close my eyes for fear I would wake up hungry and cold.

As damaging as these parental communications may have been, however, one cannot simply point an accusing finger at the communicators. For chances are high that the parents who offered their children these dubious money lessons received much the same ones from their parents before them, as did *their* parents, and on back down the line. And, to be fair, it must be added that what ends up as a neurotic, seemingly paranoid message may have started out as a realistic one.

Where a fear of poverty, for example, was a viable fear for one's forebears, the irrational residue of that fear tends to linger long after actual circumstances change. As the gentleman who reported terrors of imminent poverty told me, three out of his four grandparents actually *did* grow up in conditions where cold and hunger were not vague, menacing apparitions but brutal truths. Though he and his parents had no real need to worry, worry was woven into the family's fabric like a brightly colored thread. To tear it loose would require unraveling the cloth from which their family garb was formed.

Still and all, overtly articulated messages, no matter how patently unrealistic they may be, are often easier to grapple with than other kinds of messages. When a consistent message is conveyed in words, and where parents practice what they preach, one at least knows what one is dealing with, even though one may not like it.

Though it is no easy chore to turn down the volume of our parents' words once we have dutifully recorded them on the endlessly repeating tape of our superego, it is even more difficult to drown out nonverbally conveyed emotional messages that conflict with what is being said. Those tend to be recorded by our unconscious minds, where they linger like phantoms in the basement, affecting our thoughts and behavior as they thump and bump in the night. And as Virginia Woolf pointed out, "It is harder to kill a phantom than a reality."

To see how unspoken money messages can override spoken ones, let us look at the story of Daniel:

Now twenty-four years old, Daniel is the scion of a once very wealthy family. Though he was informed by his parents that the bulk of their Old Money was, beginning three or four generations back, mismanaged into oblivion, and though he was not raised in particularly opulent surroundings, his paternal grandparents, still in possession of the last vestiges of the family fortune, always seemed willing and able to provide certain luxurious extras. While he was growing up, there were season football tickets on the forty-yard line, tennis lessons, and Christmas vacations on tropical islands. He did not

saving. I figured they just didn't want to spoil the surprise by telling me I was going to be taken off the hook."

But Daniel's graduation came and went, as did his twenty-first birthday a few weeks later. And no trust fund materialized to meet his burgeoning needs. When he questioned his parents about it, they looked at him blankly. "What in the world," one asked him, "would ever have given you such an idea?" When he approached his grandparents and asked if they could lend him a little money so that he could make his loan payments and still take a much anticipated trip to the Far East with his girlfriend, he was turned down flat. "We just splurged on a wonderful trip for you," they chided him. "It's probably the last time we can afford to do anything like that. Do you think we're made of money? Get a job!"

In the three years since the revelation dawned on Daniel that there really was no magical reserve fund into which he could tap, he has tried to readjust to his redefined situation. He did find a job and is paying off his debt, but he feels restless at his work and somehow cheated by life. When he talks of his family, one hears the confusion and disappointment in his voice. He feels betrayed and "fooled," he says. He was never really prepared for a life of personal financial responsibility, and he finds such an existence more difficult than he might have had he been psychologically armed for it. He says that if he ever does come into a windfall—and one is left with the distinct impression that he still harbors the notion that he is entitled to it—he'd like to sail around the world. But for now he has to content himself with two weeks' vacation each year.

Daniel is well aware that he was never promised an easy ride in so many words. But the unspoken messages he'd been fed all his life contradicted virtually everything that was said on the subject of money.

We cannot simply dismiss Daniel as a spoiled, unrealistic boy who lived most of his life in a state of denial. After all, how much choice did he have? His entire family was in a state of denial.

Instead of attempting to deal with the actuality of their finite resources, they behaved as though their fortune was infinite. Instead of preserving a little of the capital that remained from their clan's ertswhile heyday, they indulged in pleasures that distracted them from the unfortunate truth that they were not really rich, after all—at least not compared to the way they might have been had things gone differently. Instead of communicating to Daniel the reality of his circumstances, i.e., that their Old Money had, as Nelson Aldrich once so elegantly phrased it, "disappeared like the Cheshire cat, leaving a smile," they instructed him on how to find the tastiest piña coladas in the tropics.

And yet once again it must be remembered that Daniel's parents and grandparents were trained in these behaviors as well. Those who controlled the family purse strings for several generations preceding them had long ago taken up residence in a financial fantasy land, where spending without thought to replenishing was the name of the game.

In the case of Daniel's family, as with so many others, the adage "Actions speak louder than words" certainly applies. To admonish one's children to "do as I say and not as I do" about money is not likely to prove an effective strategy for their education. Money is ubiquitous. We must deal with it many, many times every day. And if we have children, they will be observing those dealings. It's futile to try to disguise our true prevalent attitudes toward it by paying lip service to opposing attitudes.

As social psychologists who study cognition have long contended, it's impossible for an individual to hold two blatantly contrary beliefs in his conscious mind simultaneously. When two "truths" are in conflict, there is *cognitive dissonance*. The world doesn't jibe.

When children are presented with two competing truths,

they will doubtless pick one to cling to and distort or deny the second so that it fits in with their preferred perception.

Given the two truths "This family has no money" and "This family has money to burn," which would we be most likely to choose to believe?

CONNECTIONS AND CONCEPTIONS

If the way families behave toward money expresses their relationship to dollars and cents, it often expresses something else as well: how they feel about their relationships with one another.

At times, the way parents express their feelings toward children through money can be constructive. It is hard to fault the common practice of expressing pride and reinforcing good habits by offering a child an extra quarter or dollar for a straight-A report card, a lawn cleanly raked, a room neatly tidied. Providing that money is not the *only* way mothers and fathers let children know they care, such money messages generally do no harm. Even when children reach adulthood, parents may make small symbolic monetary offerings to them in order to let them know they are cared for.

I know a forty-year-old self-made millionaire who lives in New York City and at least once a month visits his mother in Hartford, Connecticut, where she lives in a lovely house he purchased for her. Each time he leaves his mother's house to head back to the city, she presses a twenty-dollar bill in his hand and whispers, "Here's fare for the train, son." My friend doesn't have the heart to tell her he not only doesn't need train fare but more often than not travels by limousine. He understands that her gesture has a meaning above and beyond the practical. It constitutes an offer on her part of affection, protection, and maternal concern. His unprotesting acceptance of her offer is an affectionate gesture as well. By taking the money, he preserves his mother's dignity and acknowledges her role as his nurturer. All this for twenty dollars is a bargain.

But, of course, many emotional uses of money within the context of family life can set bad precedents. Those precedents can resonate throughout a person's lifetime and, because of the way "moneygrams" work, beyond.

Money can be used to express mistrust and suspicion.

When I was little [recalls Jan, now thirty] and was sent to the store to buy groceries, my parents would always demand that I show them the receipt when I presented them with the change. Then they would count aloud and make sure that I gave them back what was coming to the penny. The same thing would happen when I was a teenager and they would give me money to buy myself a dress or a new pair of shoes. They were not ungenerous with money, but they always made me feel like I was somehow a criminal for taking it. It was sort of naturally assumed that I was trying to put one over on them, which honestly never occurred to me. I mean, why would it? But nothing seems to have changed, even though I've tried to prove myself a "respectable citizen" for the past several decades. Last year my father generously sent me two thousand dollars to open an IRA. He said he felt it was time I started planning for retirement and wanted to give me a head start. I thought it was very sweet of him, but then I read the postscript in his letter and all the old feelings came up again. "After you open an account," he wrote, "please send Mom and me a Xerox of the opening balance statement."

Money can be used to foster alliances between family members and to exclude other members.

My father was notoriously tight with money [says Peter, forty-eight], while my mother was the opposite. Though he didn't want her to work, she did earn extra money on the sly by taking in sewing and by doing some calligraphy—you know, hand-printing signs, invitations, and so forth. She was very handy and very enterprising. But my father never knew about any of her little entrepreneurial endeavors, as she was careful to confine them all to the hours when he was at the office. Naturally, though, I knew about them. And what's more, I benefited from them. Mom was always giving me money from her secret savings to buy baseball cards, comic books, candy, you know, the kinds of treats a little boy wants. But, of course, it was always, "Don't tell your father, this is just between us." I guess it was the perfect way to get me to keep her secret, because now I had secrets, too. I was a co-conspirator.

Money can instigate manipulation.

Whenever my mother wanted my father to spring for a family vacation or a new car or anything out of the ordinary that would require stretching the budget, he invariably turned her down [says Eileen, thirty-eight]. So she would coach my sister and me into coaxing him to part with the money. She would instruct us as to exactly what to say, and it usually involved making him feel embarrassed. We'd say things like, "Gee, Daddy, why can't we all go away together and have a really great time just like all our friends' families do?" It didn't always work, but it often did. If we looked coquettish enough and acted deprived enough, he'd frequently sigh and pull out his checkbook. My mother would say, "I knew you girls could do it. You're the ones he lives for." To tell you the truth, getting the vacations and the cars never seemed all that satisfying to us. We never really felt comfortable getting in the middle of our parents that way. It seemed unfair to make us do it.

And it can instigate projection and blame.

In my family, the truth was that both my parents were cheap [says Eric, twenty-six]. But neither one wanted to own up to penny-pinching in front of me and my brothers. So it was always "We can't go out to dinner, your father says we can't afford it" or "We just can't take you all to the circus. You know Mom. She claims we'll end up in the poorhouse." It seemed like whichever one we asked for something would say they wished they could give it to us. It was always the *other* one's fault that we couldn't have it. We felt like Ping-Pong balls trying to beat their system—and we never could.

Money is frequently invoked as an instrument of control.

Since I was a teenager [says Kathy, forty-three], my parents always tried to dictate who I would date by offering or withholding money. If I was dating a boy they liked, they'd say, "Here's some money, dear. Buy something pretty to wear tonight. Have your hair done!" If they disapproved of the boy, they wouldn't do that. In fact they'd say, "You know, we really wish you wouldn't go out tonight. Mrs. Smith needs a baby-sitter, and you know you've got to keep up your college fund." I must admit, it became tempting to bolster my wardrobe by seeing boys they liked.

Money can be used to foster unnatural dependencies.

When I graduated from college [says Jeanine, thirty-seven], I wanted very badly to work in the film business, which meant moving to L.A. My parents wanted me to stay in Seattle with them. I actually mustered up the courage to visit Los Angeles and go on some interviews and was offered a job as an assistant story editor at a major studio. I wanted the job badly, but it paid very little, and I had no savings with which I could even afford to relocate. My parents said they wouldn't help me to make the move. They felt I was too young to take such a step. But they promised if I stayed around and continued to live at home for a year they would start a savings account for me and add to it each month, so that in a year I could move to L.A. with no worries.

I did stay home, but at the end of a year they claimed they'd suffered a setback and needed my savings account to pull through. Just wait another year, they said. So I did that, too. But at the end of the second year, it turned out, they said, that they just hadn't been able to put enough aside. At that point I had saved enough on my own to do what I wanted and I left, despite their recriminations and warnings that I would never be able to support myself in such an unpredictable business. The only film job I could find at that point was as a low-level secretary in a studio publicity department, but I did survive and ultimately build a successful career. Still, I think I would have gotten where I am today much sooner if I'd figured out some way to start out when and where I really wanted to.

Money can be used to assuage parental guilt.

I know I give my son too much money and too many gifts [says Rose, sixty-six]. My friends all say I'm crazy for giving him half of the down payment on his new house, when I don't own a house myself and when he and his wife both have good jobs. But I

can't help myself. I feel like I owe it to him because
he had a lousy childhood and it's all my fault. When
he was little, I divorced his father, a prominent law-
yer, to marry a man I really loved. But my second
husband had no money at all. We lived very fru-
gally, and my son always had to work and go to
school at the same time. He was holding down a
million odd jobs even when he was a kid. He never
got to play Little League or join the Boy Scouts.
Now I have some money because I got a good pension plan at my company. But I don't want anything
more for myself, only for him. He deserves an easier
life. I don't need to make any changes at this stage
of the game.

And it can be offered in lieu of a heartfelt apology.

My father is a very negative man, very critical
[says Rita, thirty-two]. Often, when I tell him about
something new in my life—a new job, a new man,
he will say something derogatory. It's almost as if
he can't help himself. I try to let his comments roll
off my back. I know this is just his personality and I
should be used to his being a curmudgeon by now.
But sometimes I can't control myself, and he re-
duces me to tears. Whenever that happens, the aftermath is predictable. Within a few days there's a
check in the mail. The memo on the bottom will
read, "Congratulations on promotion" or "Take
your new beau to dinner." A while ago I simply decided to stop cashing them, which I know will drive
him to distraction when he tries to balance his
checkbook. It's the only way I can think to say,
"This just isn't good enough, Dad."

*Money can be used to express boundary problems, which
occur when family members cannot quite tell where they end
and someone else begins.*

My father was angry with me a while back [says Josh, nineteen] because I didn't pick up my sister and drive her home from a party, which I'd promised to do. I'd had to work late at my word processing job because the guy on the next shift was sick. I forgot to call my dad and tell him, since things were so hectic. He was so mad he threatened to take away my credit card—which really didn't make any sense, because it's my own account in my own name and has nothing to do with him. In fact, I pay the bills with the money I earn doing this computer work at night. I tried to explain to him that he didn't have the right to do that, and that the bank probably wouldn't let him anyhow, but that just made him madder. I think he just couldn't believe that he had no say in certain aspects of my life anymore, especially one as important as money.

My mom is always going through my purse [says Karen, sixteen], and she says she's "looking for bus change." Sometimes she takes a few quarters out, but often I don't think she takes anything at all. Besides, I know she can't possibly really need bus change, because she's a change hoarder herself. I mean there are *jars* of quarters and dimes lined up under the kitchen sink. Either she's just snooping or she wants to use something that's mine instead of using something that's hers. I just want my privacy.

Within the structure of the family, money can be used to try and achieve just about any emotional aim whatsoever. It can be used to show favoritism, as when parents shower one sibling with more financial favors than another. It can be used to try to purchase affection, as when divorced parents vie to see who can give a child more, or when monetary rewards are offered for, say, visiting one's aging grandmother. It can be used to express self-destructive tendencies, as when parents deprive themselves of even the smallest pleasures so that their children might prosper.

It can also be used to imprint gender stereotypes, as when children are given the message that "daddies take care of the money." In and of itself, this last communication accounts for an exorbitant number of destructive money attitudes in later life.

MONEY AND THE SEXES

Many adults today may recall hearing when they were young a nursery rhyme that went:

> Clap hands; clap hands till Daddy gets home;
> Daddy has money and Mommy has none.

Though such sentiments are now clearly out of step with economic and political realities, and though they may rarely be so clearly spelled out, the way that money is handled in many families still tends to foster sexist attitudes about it.

Throughout much of history, and throughout most cultures, women had very little opportunity to handle significant sums of money. Even in the wealthiest families, women tended to be merely adorned by their husbands or fathers with jewels and other emblems that served to announce "Money is nearby." Today, transgenerational traditions that ensure that decisions about how money is spent, saved, invested, or otherwise allocated fall to Dad may persist, even in two-income households where *making* money is clearly a responsibility that falls to both parents.

When children want a ruling on an allowance increase and are told, "Ask your father"; when sons are drawn into conspiracies with their mothers to withhold money-related information from Dad, lest Dad be angered that his authority is being undermined (as in the case of Peter, who had to button his lip about his mother's "secret savings"); or when daughters are coached by their mothers to charm their fathers into opening their wallets (as in the case of Eileen and her sister, who were enlisted to solicit the vacations and cars their mother desired); the emotional money association being handed down is that money equals manhood.

When little girls incorporate this message into their financial superego, they will likely find themselves financially handicapped as women. They may believe, at least on a subliminal level, that "wheeling and dealing" is a masculine domain. They may steer clear of occupations that are directly tied to the handling of money or its equivalents. They may unwittingly ignore opportunities to increase their income for fear it will make them less "feminine." They may achieve financial success only to deprive themselves of many of the pleasures of prosperity, insisting for example, "I can't possibly buy a house. I'm a single woman. I'm supposed to have a *husband* in order to do this." They may even go so far as to feel that without a man around they cannot effectively deal with rudimentary financial matters, like contributing to a retirement fund or selecting an insurance policy.

But women are not the only ones who suffer from the effects of sexist money attitudes. Little boys who are trained by their families to equate money with manhood can grow to be men who feel woefully inadequate in the presence of other men who earn more money than they. They may compulsively pursue money for the sheer pleasure of besting other men at the game. Or they may overspend money as a means of making a statement about their, shall we say, male assets.

Readers of Donald Trump's *The Art of the Deal* may recall an anecdote the ex-billionaire recounts about a visit he paid to billionaire Adnan Khashoggi. Trump notes that while he "didn't particularly care" for Khashoggi's apartment, he was impressed by the hugeness of its rooms, particularly the living room, which was the largest he'd ever seen. Inspired by his visit, Trump proceeded to take over the apartment adjacent to his own Trump Tower penthouse triplex and expand his own living room to gargantuan dimensions. "While I can't honestly say I need an eighty-foot living room," wrote the tycoon, "I do get a big kick out of having one." Well, O.K., but does anyone really think it's the size of *living rooms* we're talking about here?

Just how strongly the money-manhood equation resonates in any particular man or woman's psyche is a powerful factor in determining just how balanced or unbalanced he or she will be on the subject of money. It is yet another testament to the long-term effects of "moneygrams."

VARIATIONS ON A THEME

Of course, despite the paths that family "moneygram" messages usually take, it must be said that not *all* people merely repeat their parents' patterns when it comes to money-related behavior. Repeating what's gone before is only one way of identifying with the past. We *may* do other things instead. We may, for example, respond to parental messages by doing just the opposite of what they impart. In an all-out effort to resist becoming the adults that our mothers and fathers are, or were, we may defiantly take a stand against their attitudes by implementing attitudes that are 180 degrees opposed. We probably know people who spend much of their energy carving out a life for themselves that is a testament to their conscious rejection of their parents' lives. Perhaps they are people who have refused to wed because their parents suffered in a mutually destructive marriage. Perhaps they are people who repeatedly bend the law in response to what they perceived as their parents' overly zealous moralistic stance. Not surprisingly, money is often employed as an instrument with which to craft reactive behaviors.

Someone with parents who are financially conservative may feel compelled to take immense risks. Someone whose parents were extremely withholding may shower his own children with gifts of money. Someone whose parents insisted on taking doggie bags home from a restaurant after every meal may find himself ordering more than he can possibly consume and leaving the remains heaped on his plate simply for the satisfaction of proving to himself that he has the power to *be* himself.

The trouble with such contrary, counteractive behaviors is that they can be just as deadly a trap as pure recreations. To react for the sake of reacting is not to be oneself but to be a kind of negative print of our parents' positive image. To insist on saying "black" where they said "white" is to omit all the possibilities that lie in between the two extremes, to be blind to the many subtle shades of gray which also exist as potential ways of being.

In the movie *Wall Street*, Oliver Stone's look at the insider trading that became emblematic of 1980s avarice, it was revealed that an ambitious young would-be corporate raider, Bud Foxx, was raised by a father who clearly stated and lived by beliefs that conveyed disdain for great wealth obtained at the expense of others. The senior Foxx "never measured a man's success by the size of his wallet" and felt that money was basically a nuisance, "something you need in case you don't die tomorrow." Yet the young man he sired elevated cupidity to an art form, choosing for his mentor the unscrupulous Gordon Gekko, a man who epitomized the antithesis of his father's credo. The inevitability of Bud's downfall, one may suspect, was directly related to his compulsive determination to put as much psychological distance as possible between himself and the parental voice that continued to echo in his head.

In a variation on the reactive theme, some people feel compelled to engage in money-related behaviors which constitute an "undoing" of their parents' financial circumstances. Thus, someone whose parents more or less ignored him while they focused their energies on making a great deal of money may express a pervasive sense of emotional hurt by eschewing the womb-to-tomb financial security that is his birthright and plowing through his inheritance with unmitigated speed. ("Is it all gone yet?" asked heiress Barbara Hutton on her deathbed. She'd inherited $50 million, the equivalent of over a billion today, and left less than $3,500 behind.)

Obliterating an inheritance is a common form of "undoing," as is attempting, through one's own relentless pursuit of money, to offset the financial misfortunes or perceived inadequacies of one's parents. It would seem that at least part of what motivated Leona Helmsley, daughter of an itinerant hatmaker, and Michael Milken, whose own father spent part of his childhood in an orphanage, to so zealously pursue great wealth was a deep-seated urge to negate with a vengeance their financial legacy.

While some people seem bound and determined to undo, others seem more interested in *outdoing* their parents. If we are determined to show our parents up in the financial realm, we may spend our lives exaggerating their financial behaviors so as to feel stronger and more powerful than they. J. Paul Getty's father made millions. Getty turned it into billions because, as he said, he wanted to show his father he could.

On the other hand, if we are afraid to surpass what our progenitors have achieved, if we are paralyzed with guilt at the thought of going beyond them, we may disregard any positive messages they sent us to "do our best" and fail to live up to our true potential for fear of leaving our parents behind or "killing them off."

To complicate "moneygram" matters even further, not all sons and daughters of the same parents will necessarily exhibit the same monetary behavior. There are numerous reasons for the vast variations that can occur within one family.

It is not unusual, for example, for one child (often, though not always, the eldest) to be far more emotionally involved or "enmeshed" with the parents, to be regarded by them as an extension of themselves, and to bear the brunt of any pathology they may exhibit. Odds are high that this "chosen" child will be the one to dutifully recreate or reflexively oppose the parents' patterns and attitudes. The chosen child's sisters and brothers, being more differentiated, have a greater chance of veering off the prescribed family course.

What's more, siblings may have differing relationships with family members other than their parents—aunts, uncles, cousins, and so forth. Any relative with whom the child develops a strong attachment may end up as a powerful financial role model, perhaps one whose money messages differ radically from those of the parents.

Siblings' relationships to one another may also affect ways of dealing with money matters. H. L. Mencken defined wealth as "any income that is at least $100 more a year than the income of one's wife's sister's husband." How right he was to imply that many people define their own financial status purely as it compares to the status of those with whom they feel rivalrous.

That the accumulation of money may be symbolically used to defeat siblings is a given. Can a particularly strong urge to defeat one's brother or sisters early on in childhood foretell money-related behaviors to come? The following anecdote, another recounted by Donald Trump in *The Art of the Deal*, provides food for thought. Writing of his younger brother, Robert, Trump says:

> One day we were in the playroom of our house, building with blocks. I wanted to build a very tall building, but it turned out that I didn't have enough blocks. I asked Robert if I could borrow some of his, and he said, "Okay, but you have to give them back when you're done." I ended up using all of my blocks, and then all of his, and when I was done I'd created a beautiful building. I liked it so much that I glued the whole thing together and that was the end of Robert's blocks.

Lastly, of course, we cannot forget that within each family different money complexes may develop simply because "hand-me-down" money messages may be interpreted differently by siblings who have developed markedly different character traits. Children with particularly strong bents toward anality or orality, for example, may unconsciously arrange to screen out words and actions that don't mesh with their basic characterological framework.

Remember, the Money Complex is built layer upon layer, each one interacting with the ones above and below it. Family "moneygrams" are but one row of bricks in its towering structure, and even *they* do not comprise the whole part of our money personality that is superego.

For the superego is shaped not by parental messages alone, but also by the norms of the society in which we live. Those norms, and the cultural messages that convey them, constitute the Third Layer of the Money Complex, and the subject of the next chapter.

4
CHAPTER

. . . .

Manners,
Morals, and
Media

. . . .

Most things in life—automobiles, mistresses, cancer—are
important only to those who have them. Money, in contrast,
is equally important to those who have it and those who
don't.

—JOHN KENNETH GALBRAITH

DURING THE GREAT DEPRESSION, some 60 percent of the
American population flocked regularly to the movies. There,
visions of the well-heeled gold diggers and gangsters romping
in glamorous nightclubs and tales of ardent shoeshine boys
winning the hearts of society girls distracted them from the
harsh day-to-day realities of poverty. As Jerome Charyn puts it
in his book *Movieland:* "Being poor, America dreamed rich."

In Germantown, Pennsylvania, however, one American
was dreaming rich in a far more ingenious way. To amuse
himself in the hours between whatever odd jobs he could find
to help him feed his family, Charles B. Darrow, an unemployed
heating engineer, invented a board game called Monopoly.

The object of Monopoly was, of course, to propel one's
token around the streets of Atlantic City (the resort town
where the Darrow clan had vacationed in more prosperous
times) in hopes of accruing real estate. The game offered each
of its players equal opportunity to acquire inviting little green
houses and imposing red hotels, to pile up comforting stacks of
bogus bills, and to collect two hundred dollars simply for pass-

ing *Go*. It offered them, in short, a very different world from the one they were living in.

In the world of Monopoly, the bank never went broke. If it ran out of money, the rules stipulated, the banker could issue as much as was needed simply by inscribing currency amounts on blank pieces of paper. Wow. In the world of Monopoly, bad luck existed, all right, but so did the ever-present prospect that good luck might overcome it in a flash, just like in the movies!

Monopoly represented a financial fantasy come true. Darrow tapped into his down-and-out countrymen's wish for the return of their vanished financial security blanket. And the public responded accordingly. Despite Parker Brothers' initial reluctance to manufacture the game (it was too complicated, they said, and took too long to play), it was rapidly to become their hottest-selling diversion of all time.

Today, Monopoly ranks as the world's most popular board game. Published in an astonishing number of languages, it continues to be a source of amusement wherever it is played. What's more, for the millions who play it in dozens of countries and cultures, it is also a source of social money education.

Born of one man's fantasy which was a reaction to a real economic condition, i.e., depression, Monopoly came to embody a collective fantasy and later to evolve into a cultural imperative. Make money, the game exhorts. Then make more still. For the more you get, the more is yet to come.

For many children in the lands where Monopoly is played, to play the game is to make a first acquaintance with capitalistic concepts like *mortgage* and *stock, title deed* and *bankruptcy*. Along with its practical lessons, the game offers emotional ones. Whether triumph or defeat is the outcome of one's competitive endeavors, it is almost impossible to play the game without experiencing money-related anxiety, dread, and near-drooling desire.

Almost impossible—but not entirely. For there exists a place where Monopoly's acquisitive message is drowned out by alternate messages that resound far more loudly. That place is in the desert of northern Mexico, at an isolated ranch that goes by the name of Comunidad los Horcones. At this ranch, residents make a concerted effort to maintain a society based strictly on the behaviorist principles of B. F. Skinner's novel-cum-treatise *Walden Two*. The community's underlying philosophy is that humans can be taught to peacefully coexist, cooperate, and share. To promote the ideal of sharing, los Horcones's elaborate code of "behavioral objectives" decrees that no individual wages shall be paid, that all money earned by members of the community is community property, and that all spending decisions are put to a vote after discussion.

According to *The New York Times*, it is with "some pride" that residents recall what happened when the children of los Horcones were introduced to the ubiquitous Parker Brothers board game. "Instead of trying to drive each other into bankruptcy, the young players offered to lend money to each other so everyone could be wealthy."

What happened here? Didn't these kids get the *point?* One assumes they got it, of course. But what they observe and are taught on a daily basis is that in their society, the "point" of Monopoly is beside the point.

SOCIETY SPEAKS

The money messages of any given society resonate throughout that society and, like the messages of one's parents, they embody the kind of formidable authority that is rarely ignored. The attitudes, opinions, and very often the ambitions we formulate in relation to money are strongly influenced by our particular environment and cultural milieu. Thus is the Third Layer of the Money Complex formed.

The Third Layer of the Money Complex is built onto a foundation of First Layer primal metaphors and Second Layer family dynamics. Society is, after all, a collection of families, and families are collections of individuals. Thus, society's commands and prohibitions often reflect a shared perception of common experiences that originally occurred on an intrapsychic level and that were perhaps echoed, even embellished, in family life.

In certain ways, it is difficult to determine precisely where our parents' money messages leave off and society's begin. After all, it is because children are born to a particular set of parents that they find themselves in the city or the country, in America or China or Bangladesh, on a kibbutz or in the suburbs. Besides, parents are cultural ambassadors of the world they inhabit, the first channels through which society's messages are delivered. It is, in a sense, their job to bring the outside in to their offspring.

But society's money messages are transmitted via other avenues as well.

What's rich and what's poor? That may depend, for you, on where you grew up, where you went to school, or what your neighbors did for a living. To those with little money, each piece of it can seem worth infinitely more. In fact, in a study of the perception of money, where children from lower economic brackets were asked to draw pictures of various coins, they sketched them significantly larger than those from wealthy families.

How should money be made? That may depend on what church you belong to, what television shows you watch, on whether all the "good kids" in your neighborhood had paper routes when you were twelve.

On what should "disposable income" be spent? Fine dining? A really good bowling ball? How about sailing? That may depend on whether your friends consider the pastime of sailing tantamount to standing in the shower ripping up fifty-dollar bills or whether you fraternize with the sort of folks who learned to sail in the gene pool.

What should you wear, eat, or drive if you want to appear "well-to-do"? "Plano" power glasses with nonprescription lenses? Saris with golden threads? Chanel suits and Reeboks? Ten-gallon Stetsons? That all depends.

Someone who grows up in a capitalist society will think about money and money equivalents differently from someone who grows up in a socialist society. Someone who grows up in the lower socioeconomic classes will obviously have a different perspective from one who is raised amid the middle and upper classes. And someone who grows up in a society where passage from one class to another is possible will surely have a different outlook from one who lives in a world where being born into a given class most likely means staying there, no matter what.

A person who grows up in a small town or rural environment, where, as Thorstein Veblen noted, "everybody's affairs, especially everybody's pecuniary status, are known to everybody else," may well have a different relationship to money from his urban counterpart. If nothing else, he will feel far less temptation to display his financial status through ostentatious "conspicuous consumption." Ostrich-skin briefcases and $1,100 suits don't carry much weight in America's Corn Belt. And what's the point of showing off a new Mercedes coupe if the guys at the barbershop know you haven't made the last two payments on your tractor?

The era during which one grows up can also have a significant impact on the molding of one's money attitudes. As psychohistorians have noted, prevailing social attitudes toward money tend to move in cycles, occurring and recurring throughout the centuries.

Growing up in the fiscally flamboyant 1980s—where money-as-food was the overriding collective metaphor, and paying excessive attention to getting and spending was socially sanctioned—imbued a far different set of norms and values than coming of age in the 1930s. And growing up in the 1990s, this "morning-after" decade in which it has become fashionable to be somewhat embarrassed about the binges of the decade before, and when guilt and shame—the "downside" feelings associated with money—seem to be reactivating, will mean something else again.

As we undergo the passage from childhood through adolescence through young adulthood and even on into adulthood itself, the social layer of our money personality is shaped by lessons garnered from fictitious and celebrity role models, secular and religious teachers, from friends and peers, and from the carefully constructed messages of advertisers and marketers.

HEROES AND ANTI-HEROES

The celebrity factor can have a considerable influence on how we think about money. Since the beginning of community life, mankind has focused much of its collective attention on those who perform courageous physical or spiritual acts, such as saving a life or delivering missives from the gods. But since money's inception, society has also tended to count among its most notorious members those people who have a special relationship to lucre. Financial voyeurism gives us a vicarious thrill.

In contemporary American culture, we like to hear and read about real or imaginary people who somehow managed to accrue a lot of money. In the '80s, we looked to them to learn how to get it and how to spend it. As that decade drew to a close, the nonfiction and fiction tomes that topped *The New York Times* best-seller list were, respectively, *The Art of the Deal* and *Bonfire of the Vanities*. (The latter was, of course, Tom Wolfe's hilarious depiction of a world in which the well-heeled routinely paid $150 a person to pick at esoteric pastas at the "restaurant of the century," a dining establishment so devoted to overpriced pampering that waiters cheerfully skipped over a corpse to deliver dinner before it got soggy.) As we turned the corner into the '90s, some of our well-heeled heroes became anti-heroes. We gobbled up news and tabloid tips and righteous editorials on the "fall of Trump," the tax trials of Leona Helmsley, and the sentencing of junk-bond king Michael Milken. And we employed our anti-heroes to reassure ourselves that we would never behave as they behaved—for, after all, look where it got them.

We like to compare ourselves and our own money morals to real and make-believe folk who are perceived to embrace noble attitudes toward money and to those who it is generally agreed, at least in public, have unsavory attitudes toward it. What's more, we like to compare our money manners to those whose relationship to their financial circumstances is generally acknowledged to be irrational and inappropriate. Those who grew up watching the popular TV situation comedies "Green Acres" and "The Beverly Hillbillies," for example, doubtless whiled away many an evening chortling at the Park Avenue couple who renounced the life of the Manhattan wealthy to cavort with hogs and roosters down on the farm, and at silly Jed Clampett and his kinfolk, who, despite their cache of "bubblin' crude" and their elaborate mansion and "cement pond," never learned to affect the properly superior affectations of the well-to-do.

The harebrained get-rich-quick schemes of Ralph Kramden and Lucy Ricardo, along with the hyperbolic avariciousness of "Taxi" 's Louis DePalma, whose fondest dream is to "get naked and roll around" in a heap of hundred-dollar bills, are also a source of hilarity—and, in their way, of instruction as well. They teach us how *not* to act toward money if we ourselves do not wish to be the butt of jokes and general derision.

Money lessons imparted by famous and infamous public personages and fictional characters impact on the attitudes of all of us. For children, however, they can be especially salient, providing an internal standard against which they will long measure themselves.

Of course, if a child is not intrigued by a celebrity or amused by a make-believe character, he generally has the option of tuning his message out merely by switching off the television or radio, or laying a book or magazine aside. At school, however, tuning out is not so easy. And it is at school that a number of other monetary "shoulds" and "shouldn'ts" are also communicated in formal and informal ways.

CLASSROOMS AND CLASS

Formal financial education in school, when it is available, tends to emphasize the money norms and values that the collective conscience of a society deems most laudable. In America today, one of the "shoulds" we learn in school is that "one should save."

In School Savings Programs, which gained popularity in the 1950s and '60s and are enjoying a resurgence today, students learn to make deposits in their own accounts, to decipher bank statements, and to calculate the interest they will earn. But that's not all they learn. Written syllabus materials that go along with the School Savings curriculum, all bearing the U.S. Department of Education seal of approval, could not make it any clearer that, in theory at least, hanging on to one's money is a "should," whereas spending it is a "shouldn't."

Booklets explaining the rudiments of banking are illustrated with drawings of a handsome clean-cut boy smilingly turning his allowance over to a teller and proudly surveying a computer screen which informs him his savings have appreciated by the sum of two dollars. In not-so-subtle contrast to him, a disheveled thuglike youth sporting a belt buckle reading "Zero" is shown gleefully emptying a cookie jar full of coins onto his bedroom floor and bragging, "I'm going to spend my interest as soon as it's posted to my account." Lest the message be missed, the pamphlet is also populated by a hypermuscular superhero type who mouths slogans like "I pity the person who doesn't save" and "I pity the person who tries to take more out of their account than they have in it."

As children progress to higher grade levels, additional School Savings materials, in the form of booklets with titles like *How to Make a Million,* move from explaining the ins and outs of simple passbook savings accounts to more sophisticated investment concepts, from CDs and money market funds to stocks, bonds, and T-bills. Though the object of these advanced lessons is to impart strategies that lead to profit making, emphasis is still placed on security and prudence. It is the aforementioned clean-cut boy who favors treasury bills and blue chip stocks. His reckless, thuglike alter-ego laments, "I could afford to get my ears pierced if I hadn't lost my money on pork bellies."

Should all this emphasis on fiscal responsibility make students nervous, teachers may also obtain from the American Banking Association and from the Big Daddy of banks, the Federal Reserve itself, a host of comic-book-like tracts with titles like *Meet the Bank* and *Once Upon a Dime* designed to head money-related anxiety off at the pass. In language filled with jolly banking puns ("The teller can tell you that.") and with drawings of cheerful anthropomorphic money characters (Charley Check and Red Cent), these convivial comics aim to instruct youngsters of all ages in the fundamentals of the U.S. banking system, offering assurance that the elaborate institutions that create and manage our money are trustworthy, responsive, and, beyond that, downright friendly. The message: One should have faith in the economy. (An important message from a social standpoint. For, as we shall see in a later chapter, without faith there can be no economy.)

Most family credit counselors and child psychologists think there's a lot to be said for offering formal money management education in the schools. They are emphatic in their belief that communicating the basics of finance to children will go a long way toward easing their transition to independent adulthood. Given the fact that when polled by ABC News shortly after the Crash of '87, a random sample of Americans who had already reached adulthood scored an average grade of only 46 percent on an economics quiz whose questions included "What is the New York Stock Exchange?" and "What is the Dow Jones Industrial Average?" such education can clearly begin none too soon.

Yet, formal money education has its problems and its crit-

100

ics. Some say it may be unrealistic to try to teach children to save for long-range abstract goals. Indeed, developmental psychologists point out that it is often not until a youngster has reached fourteen or fifteen years of age that he possesses a real ability to plan for the future.

Some have also criticized educational literature aimed at children for being overly simplistic and idealistic. Children's school lessons on banking do not tend to dwell on, say, the savings and loan debacle. Likewise, their lessons on the stock and commodities markets include few, if any, caveats regarding the persistent follies engendered by crowd psychology.

Yet it must be remembered that the goal of formal money education in school is to impart "should" and "shouldn't" messages, not "is" and "isn't" messages. If the object is to instill a fine upstanding money conscience in students, it stands to reason that the values stressed will be free of cynicism.

But a different sort of omission is also noticeable in structured school money lessons. *Nowhere does attention seem to be paid to the emotional element of financial life.* It is never taught formally, for example, that the presence or absence of money can affect the way that people act toward others and feel about themselves.

That lesson is learned at school, to be sure, but it is not learned in the classrooms. It is learned in cafeterias, in playgrounds, in parking lots, hallways, and locker rooms. And it is taught not by teachers but by a child's own peers.

THE COMPULSION TO COPY

Veblen wrote that the "propensity for emulation" is one of the strongest and most persistent financial motives. What he meant was simply that people like to copy other people—especially other people who have more money than they.

Plato says that "poverty consists not so much in small property as in large desires." Many of us, regardless of how much money our own families possessed, had our desires for *more* money and *more* of the things it can buy stoked by class-mates who were driven to school in snazzier cars, who wore finer clothes and had bigger allowances to spend on coveted lunchtime snacks. For many of us first learned at school that money is associated with pecking order and popularity.

During school years, children want nothing so badly as to fit in, to conform. Should their financial status fail to live up to that of the kids who are generally acknowledged as the ones to emulate, they may come to know resentment, envy, and shame—and to begin to consciously attach these feelings to money. Though none of their official lesson plans said so, they begin to understand that no matter how diligently they tend to their School Savings account, they probably won't be perceived as cool (or whatever the equivalent of "cool" is in their particular school's lingo) unless they are wearing the right, i.e., expensive and status-related, pair of sneakers.

Tom Wolfe has commented that "status is fundamental, an inescapable part of human life." Indeed, throughout life we are exquisitely status-conscious. Even in eras when everyone, across the board, makes do with less, some people always have more than others. We know who these people are, how they live, and we assuage feelings of social inadequacy by fashioning our outer selves after those who are higher up the financial ladder.

Most of us are well aware of what signifies the presence of status and, therefore, of money in our particular community. In American culture, for example, adults have in recent times associated wealth with thinness, with suntans, with various domestic habits, and even with certain color preferences. Social critic Paul Fussell points out in his book *Class* that the presence or absence of money can be conveyed through such subtle cues as where people place their television set (the higher up the socioeconomic scale you go, the less likely you are to have a tube in your living room) and what time dinner is served (the higher up one goes, the longer one delays the evening meal). Carlton Wagner, head of the Wagner Institute for Color Research, notes that those in the upper socioeconomic strata favor darker, more complex colors (burgundy, garnet, forest green), while those in the lower strata gravitate toward simpler, brighter shades (grass green, sky blue, fire-engine red). Most people in our society know these things, even if they don't know they know them. One need comprehend nothing about color theory to appreciate that a man in a brown suit and an orange tie emits a different money message from one sporting a charcoal gray suit and a forest green tie with a whisper of cobalt. And one need not hold a Ph.D. in sociology to intuit that someone who eats dinner on a living-room snack table at 6 P.M. while watching "Bowling for Dollars" probably has less income than someone who dines in a dining room at 9 P.M. and deigns to watch television only from bed, and then only "Masterpiece Theatre."

Parents who wonder why children who seemed perfectly content with their lot in life disembark from their school bus one day making plaintive requests for items outside the scope of the family budget, or evincing new upwardly mobile mannerisms or preferences for things they never liked before, must realize that the inevitable process of monetary social pressure and money-related stratification has already begun.

The informal messages learned at school have hit their mark, and their children have registered the following cultural lessons: Not having as much money as your friends can make you feel bad, rejected, outcast. (Not having money is, therefore, a "shouldn't.") Having it can make you feel good, empowered, affiliated. (Having money is, therefore, a "should.") But if having money is good, acting like you have it can often be just as good. Purchase and pretense can often equal social prestige. It can also be a "should," therefore, to let one's financial aspirations and affectations get ahead of one's finances.

Many parents, of course, may not be wholly enthused about children embracing this particular message. They can try to mitigate their children's desire for socioeconomic conformity by countering it with messages of their own. They may refuse to buy overpriced trendy fashions, even though the resulting tantrum may take a heavy toll on domestic harmony. Or they may try explaining that uniqueness can sometimes be more rewarding than mindless conformity. (In parentspeak: "If everyone else were jumping off a bridge, would you do it, too?") But whatever their tactics, there is not much they can do to prevent the message from getting through in the first place. In our society, if reinforcement of the compulsion to copy doesn't come from one sphere, it will likely come from another.

FIVE THOUSAND MESSAGES A DAY

Nowadays, even if mothers and fathers were to yank their sons and daughters out of school and lock them up with a governess in a tower deep in the forest, they would still have to contend with a profusion of messages touting economic me-too-ism. They would, that is, if this hypothetical tower came equipped with a television set or if the governess took her charges on occasional excursions to the local Forest Mall.

In modern market societies, someone always stands to make money through the application of social pressure to spend money. Today, the potential to make money from children is greater than ever, and advertisers and marketers obviously know it.

Children are growing into a major consumer force. In America alone, they spend over $4.2 billion a year. Even children from households with modest incomes today generally have some discretionary funds at their command. It should come as no surprise then that more and more advertising is being directly targeted at kids.

Advertising is nothing new. Even in ancient Egypt, stone tablets inscribed with the sales messages of merchants were strategically placed along well-traveled roads. But over the centuries, advertisers have become increasingly sophisticated about what motivates people to part with their money. Ad messages used to say, "Buy this. It's here." Then they said,

"Buy this. It's good." Then they said, "Buy this, it's good *for* you." But *now* they say, "Buy this so you can be like the people who have already bought it. *They* are good. If you do what they do, *you* will appear to be good, too."

Increasingly, market research backs up Veblen's contention about emulation with hard facts and figures. It documents the fact that adults purchase consumer goods, from sports cars to polo shirts, because they identify, or wish to identify, with the kind of people they think drive or wear them. The same principle applies in an even more pronounced way to children and adolescents. The reason they want Teenage Mutant Ninja Turtle whatnots or a particular brand of blue jeans is because, in their eyes, "anyone who is anyone" already owns them and because those who do not own them risk blatant ostracism by their peers.

Because of youngsters' developmental need to perceive themselves as part of the crowd, because of their palpable terror at the thought of being misfits, they comprise a population whose social insecurities are especially easy to exploit. But few people in this culture are immune to this dynamic or are likely to become so.

Today, a relentless barrage of ads aimed at both children and adults fills the airwaves day and night. What's more, "alternative media" ads are showing up in books, in high school classrooms, in games, in public restrooms, on parking meters, and in the Muzak tapes that play in elevators, supermarkets, and department stores. Incredibly, it is now estimated that the average consumer is bombarded each day with over five thousand advertising messages.

It sometimes seems as though every nook and cranny of daily life, every split second of existence is being filled up with commercials. The ones that will exert the strongest tug on our heartstrings and our purse strings are, more likely than not, the ones that offer us the tantalizing fantasy that obeying their message will allow us to buy ourselves an identity we find appealing.

MONEY SACRIFICE

Along with money messages emanating from profit-seeking quarters, our monetary superegos must also integrate messages emanating from nonprofit quarters, both religious and secular. From the time of Sunday school and Halloween UNICEF drives on, instructions in giving are an inextricable part of our social money education.

"Give" messages do not conflict with getting, spending, and saving messages so much as they complement them. Like other parts of our personalities, the social superego consists of opposites bonding together to form a whole. It embraces conflict and multiple possibilities. We should want to get money and use it to buy things, it tells us. But we should want to donate it as well.

Yet the prospect of giving raises many questions. For example, to whom should we give, and what should we give?

Even before money per se became an integral part of society, humans gave valuables to gods on a routine basis. In the course of history, countless numbers of animals, comely virgins, and even human hearts were sacrificed at altars all across the world (the reasoning being, it would seem, that divinities are naturally preoccupied with the same concerns that preoccupy humans and that they prize what we prize). At a certain point, worshippers began offering the gods clay images of beasts containing valuable objects. This, anthropologists suspect, was the origin of the piggy bank!

Today, of course, the valuable object that people sacrifice is money itself. Though giving money is far less theatrical, not to mention less messy and less potentially lethal, than primitive sacrifice, many people still give with the intent of benefiting the deity they worship, or the earthly representation of that deity. Mormons, for example, tithe 10 percent of their income to the Church of Latter Day Saints. Followers of Oral Roberts showered him with $8 million so the Lord would not make good on his threat to "call him home."

Oftimes, however, the giving instructions to which we are exposed, at church, at charity benefits, via public service announcements and mail and phone solicitations, simply instruct us to be philanthropical. They exhort us to give money to the neediest in the community, to deserving fellow men, and to various worthwhile social, political, and environmental causes.

Most of us, albeit to varying degrees, like to comply with "give" messages. There is certainly immense social pressure to give, and those who do not are often ashamed to admit to their lack of compliance with this cultural dictum. But another interesting question is: How did giving money and money equivalents away—especially in light of how much emphasis we put on getting them—ever become a dictum in the first place? If "give" messages prove so effective, it must be because they tap into universal elements of the psyche.

One reason we like to give is because doing so helps us to expiate feelings of guilt, to atone for our perceived indulgences, transgressions, and sins. As we have already seen, part of our psyche associates money with what is worst in us, with what is the most unclean. Giving money, or gifts that obviously cost money, helps us as a society to symbolically rid ourselves of its stain. Small wonder the '90s are being hailed as the era of "new altruism." As a culture, we are doing penance for the sins of the '80s.

We give also to alleviate feelings of anxiety and fear. When televangelist Jimmy Swaggart in 1987 wrote to his followers, "If I have to cancel just one station because I don't get your support, then people will die and go to hell by the thousands," he touched a powerful nerve. Obviously not everyone responds well to the Swaggart approach, but many of us have to a certain extent incorporated the biblical question "What doth it profit a man to gain the world and lose his soul?" into our monetary superego. If the mere donation of dollars here and there can serve as a kind of insurance against afterlife hellfire or equivalent torment in this lifetime, why take a chance?

Beyond all this, there is yet another powerful incentive to

give. The noted anthropologist Marvin Harris has pointed out that the reason humans made sacrifices to the gods was in order to effect trades. In exchange for what they offered to the heavens, he says, "people expected to receive goods and services from the spirit world." Goods like food, sunshine, and the right amount of rain. Services like protection from rival tribes and man-eating tigers. Sacrifice became a kind of investment. People offered something valuable in the belief that something even more valuable would come back to them.

Today, superego instructions still allude to the concept of reciprocity. "To give is to receive," they say. Of course, some of us take the message more literally than others. Before being convicted of twenty-four fraud and conspiracy counts in federal court, Jim Bakker urged his devotees to give to the PTL ministry and implied they might expect earthly prosperity in return. "If you pray for a camper," he would remind the faithful, "be sure to tell Him what color." But even those who are not so naive as to anticipate the arrival of Winnebagos on a quid pro quo basis in exchange for their acts of generosity realize on some level that giving generally nets them *something*.

Often the benefits we receive in exchange for giving are feelings. Feelings of self-esteem and worthiness, of security and safety. Feelings of being deserving of what we ourselves have already been given. Through giving, and through teaching our children to give, we make an investment in our peace of mind. It is a worthwhile investment, to be sure.

The fact that we give at least partially if not entirely out of an impulse to ease our own social or psychic distress does not make giving any less valuable. If the by-products of that "self-serving" impulse result in the smoothing out of economic inequities, so much the better. If we give a dollar to a homeless man because on some level we imagine that by doing so the fates may spare us *his* fate, at least the homeless man has a dollar more than he did before.

If we were exposed solely to getting and saving and spending messages, we would likely view any parting with money on behalf of others as self-deprivation. "Giving" messages help open us to another perspective, i.e., that the act of willingly parting with money—in order that it may be used to benefit others—can be a means of self-enhancement.

. . . .

Certainly, "giving" messages—like all social messages—can be overdone. How many of us have come home to find our mailbox stuffed with pleas to save a whale, conserve a rain forest, preserve public television, help elect a congressman, help educate a child? What will we do? With how many requests will we comply? Which ones will activate our social superego? That, of course, depends on many things. It depends on what those around us think is a worthy cause and on how much we want them to think well of us for supporting something that is dear to them. But it depends also on the priorities we learned at our parents' knees and on the primal metaphors our individual psyches may embrace.

Indeed, when it comes to money, society's dictums often reflect the dictums of the psyche. When a society advocates getting and spending as the answer to life's frustrations, it reinforces infantile oral conflicts and feelings of greed and envy. When it conveys to its members that money can be used to bolster self-image or given away to alleviate fear, it reinforces the use of money as a security blanket. When it issues imperatives to save, it reinforces anal tendencies and withholding behavior. When it invokes guilt and shame to activate the superego, it does so by reinforcing the unconscious equation that linked shame and money in the first place: that of money and excrement.

Society's money messages are, in a way, echoes and embellishments of the drives, desires, and denials of each one of us. And so, as we shall see in the next chapter, are society's means of handling the financial transactions of everyday life.

5

. . . .

Reality Checks

. . . .

Money is not green engraved paper, it is a blinking light in a computer, a shouted fraction between two traders on a phone who never had a day of Economics 141. The money moves faster than the rules of any institution or any one government.

—ADAM SMITH

The techniques of money, like other techniques, are . . . a response to express, insistent, and often-repeated demands.

—FERNAND BRAUDEL

EVERY DAY, as a matter of course, the vast majority of us engage in money exchange. We pull into gas stations, sit down in restaurants and cafes, poke around hardware stores. There, we ascertain the price of an item—a quart of oil, a carafe of wine, a new faucet for the kitchen sink—and if we want it at that price, pay. A specific agreement has been reached between buyer and seller.

Yet, though we do not consciously stop to think about it, whenever we exchange money we are making a far broader agreement. Money has value because everyone in a given society believes it does. To engage in a monetary transaction with someone is, in effect, to say, "This money encompasses me and you and our willingness to abide by the same reality."

But how should this ritual of reality consensus be expressed in conceptual terms? How should we pay for what we buy? What instruments and methods shall we employ? Shall we fork over cash or, more likely, write a check or flash a credit card? How will our choice of method make us feel about the money we've spent?

The techniques and technology of money are inextricably bound up in money attitudes. The ways in which our culture creates money, represents money, and moves money around affect the way we conceptualize money—and, thus, the way we react to it. It is our emotional reactions to the technology of money that shape the Fourth Layer of the Money Complex.

CASH—THE LAST FOUR-LETTER WORD

One February night, I worked late researching an article at a library on Manhattan's East Side and then made my way by bus to my apartment on the West Side. Somewhere in the course of that evening, either while I was engrossed in my fact-finding or while perusing a magazine article on the bus bound for home, I was, without realizing it, relieved of both the credit card case and checkbook I carried in my purse.

After experiencing the requisite rage and anxiety that routinely befall the victim of such events, I began the tedious process of damage containment. I dialed the appropriate 800 numbers and informed the necessary parties that certain items had been "lost or stolen." That night, I tossed and turned, fervently hoping that I had forestalled the worst and planning my strategy for the day ahead.

The following morning, I headed straight off to my bank, closed out my checking account, and ordered checks for a new one. I then made my way to a midtown department store to replace the credit card case that had vanished, eagerly anticipating the day when all its contents—MasterCard, Visa, American Express, department store and gasoline charge plates, and an automated teller machine activator card—would again be nestled snugly inside.

Having just visited my bank, I was armed with several fifty-dollar bills. But when I handed one to the salesperson, she eyed me suspiciously.

"Is this all you have?" she asked.

"I'm afraid so."

"Don't you have one of our charge cards?"

"Sorry."

"No credit cards of any kind?" The tone of her voice was such that I felt compelled to explain my impropriety.

"Well," I babbled compliantly, "you see, I normally have lots of credit cards. Lots. Really. But they were stolen last night. Which is why I'm buying this credit card case, you see."

The salesclerk's eyes went limpid with compassion, for I was now a recognizable and reputable being, fully capable of provoking empathy. But still, she lamented, she could not help me. The store had just opened and she could not make change from her register. Nor could she take any of the temporary checks I had acquired earlier at the bank, for they did not have my name and address printed on them, and besides, when accepting checks, the store required—what else—credit cards as I.D. However, she added optimistically, if I were to break the fifty into smaller bills—and perhaps they could assist me in doing so at the gloves or notions counter—we would be in business.

Game for anything, I set off on my mission. I was, in fact, turned down by both gloves and notions, but I got lucky in scarves. Soon I was armed with both a virgin credit card holder and some small bills to boot. It was now time to get back to my real-life agenda, which necessitated a stop at an overnight package delivery office to send off a letter that absolutely, positively had to get to San Francisco. Alas, it was not long before I discovered that the delivery service did not take cash.

"No cash?" I asked. "Never?"

That's right. None. Never.

I realized it was going to be a long day. I was, however, consoled by the fact that, thankfully, I did not have to rent a car or purchase an airline ticket. Attempting to do either of those things without credit cards would, as we know, have proved Kafkaesque.

Several more days passed before my financial life was more or less restored to its "normal" state, and in that time I experienced a number of unpleasant emotions. More than a few people gave me curious glances—or at least so I imagined—when I paid for items in hard currency. I felt disconnected, invalidated, somehow embarrassed.

In a country where 75 percent of all purchases are paid for by credit card or check (and where that percentage is likely to increase as more and more fast food chains and movie theaters are cheerfully accepting payment by plastic), what's normal is to deal less and less with actual dollars and cents and more and more with less tangible, more abstract forms of lucre.

. . . .

Throughout history, the techniques of money exchange and the representative forms money itself has taken have changed radically. As they have changed, our notion of financial "realities" has changed.

No one can deny that contemporary manifestations of money and credit in their highly abstract forms serve many practical functions. Without checks and instruments of credit at our command, our roads would be gridlocked with armored trucks stuffed with cash currency or gold bricks. Without electronic records, commerce as we know it would grind to a halt.

Yet one cannot help but wonder what other purpose money in its most modern manifestations achieves. Aside from fulfilling practical demands, what psychological ones does it fulfill? To discern the answer to this question, we must know something of money's history.

SHELLS, COINS, PAPER, PLASTIC

Over the course of centuries, the more sophisticated and complex civilizations became, the more intangible were the monetary instruments they employed.

Long ago, before money as we know it came into being, various tokens of wealth, which historians call archaic money, played a role in tribal societies. When tribal leaders performed ceremonies or when medicine men sang healing chants, they might be reimbursed for their efforts with items which the tribespeople concurred had a more or less fixed value.

Those "things" with which they were "paid" were things of the sea and things of the earth, transformed by human craft and artistry into money artifacts. On the shores of Africa, *zimbos*, which are small sea-snail shells, and *cowries*, small blue-and-red-streaked seashells, were threaded on strings and used as currency objects. Necklaces of dogs' teeth and arm bands of feathers were also forms of money, as were *lubongos*, pieces of handwoven cloth about as large as a sheet of typing paper, used in sets of ten. The Indians of North America used wampum, tiny strung cylinders cut from blue or violet seashells. In Tibet, coral adornments served as a kind of money. The Yap Islanders of the Pacific constructed giant money wheels made of stone.

Within certain African societies, handcrafted artifacts of iron, bronze, and copper, often so arrestingly beautiful even by modern standards that we view those still preserved today as precious works of art—and pay thousands of dollars for them— were customarily offered as payment in important economic transactions, such as wife-buying. Some of the metal objects were tiny and were also worn as jewelry, especially bracelets and anklets. Others were appreciated simply as sculptures of fanciful shapes, often inspired by the shapes of weapons or tools. (In a review of a gallery showing of African currency objects, *New York Times* art critic Rita Reif described the artifacts as resembling, among other things, "miniature iron banners, copper croquet wickets, a bronze spiral from a giant's bedspring [and] iron spearheads too thin to penetrate more than air.") While not functionally useful, these objects represented the time, effort, and skill of their makers and were made of materials that were themselves prized.

Indigenous archaic currencies worked very well in isolated societies. But as the world changed, as societies became less isolated, and as economic dealings became more complicated, archaic money was doomed to extinction. Heavy twining sculptures of bronze are hardly the sort of monetary instruments to which the advice "Don't leave home without them" handily applies.

Increasingly, modern social orders and new circumstances required—indeed demanded—convenience. Money had to be in a form that could be moved and moved fast. In widely separated societies at varying times, coinages were instituted to accomplish movement and to solve certain other practical problems.

In Greece in the eighth century B.C., and in Rome in the fifth century B.C., standardized coinage—imprinted coins of uniform purity and weight backed by state authority—came into usage. Easily transportable, durable, and fungible (i.e., divisible into smaller and smaller parts and exchangeable for equivalent units) coins facilitated trade by replacing awkward barter systems. It proved far more convenient to swap a sack of money for material goods than to coax one's bellowing livestock to market and there face the prospect of endless haggling over how many pigs equal a bushel of wheat and how many sheep rate a pound of saffron.

Ultimately, of course, even coins proved too cumbersome to keep the money engine running up to speed. By the Middle Ages, travel was becoming more and more common. The weight of coins rendered them impractical, and, besides, travelers were afraid they might be stolen. Instead, those about to take to the road visited goldsmiths who exchanged their coins for receipts. When they reached their destination, they went to the shop of another designated goldsmith and in exchange for the surrendered receipts procured coins once again. In time, the second step was eliminated. Rather than withdraw the actual coins at their journey's end, people found it more convenient to use their receipts to pay debts and make purchases. This was, in effect, paper money at work—but paper money different from the kind we now know. (Each note of our currency consists of information designating its purchasing power, but the note in itself is not valuable. It does not represent a claim on actual silver or gold.)

About the same time that people began paying for things with receipts, another monetary custom arose. They began to pay their bills with letters that instructed goldsmiths to pay coins to the bearers of the letters. These letters were, in effect, early forms of checks. Proper checks, i.e., checks drawn on individual accounts, came into use in England toward the middle of the eighteenth century. Today, we make most of our payments in checkbook money. There are over 125 million checking accounts in the United States alone, and the roles of coin and currency have been reduced accordingly.

Andy Warhol, the pop artist who made much of his fondness for hard cash and frequently confessed his inability to comprehend anything but "green bills," was known to complain that "checks aren't money." In a way he was right. Checkbook money does not exist as hard currency. Though banks are obliged to make good on checks written by their customers up to the amount in the accounts of those customers, it would be wrong to conceptualize the balance listed at the bottom of one's checking account statement as a sackful of greenbacks sitting in the bank's basement vault. Banks are required by the Federal Reserve to hold on to only a fraction of deposits. They lend and invest the rest and in the process expand checkbook money many times over. Meanwhile, the bulk of the money in our personal accounts exists in the form of electronic records and computer entries.

Just as checks made it possible to bypass the handling of actual money, so does the use of credit cards. By wielding rectangles of plastic, we can "charge" our purchases, receive itemized monthly statements, and pay what we owe by putting a check in the mail. In the future, it is likely that money's forms will continue to change, with more and more sophisticated types of electronic transfers holding sway. Perhaps, some speculate, someday we will never have reason to manipulate so much as a nickel. Perhaps each of us will have one central credit file, and the file will be debited each time we spend.

What we have contrived to do, it seems, and what we wish

to continue to do, is to divorce money from any intrinsic value whatsoever. We have made money less representative of the natural world and of human artistry, less of an integrated and organic part of our existence. Ironically, the ways in which we have fashioned the "reality" that is money have served to make money less and less "real." But why should this be so?

A classical Freudian, focused solely on money's excremental aspects, would answer that question by saying humans are trying to "clean up" money. In a paper called "The Ontogenesis of the Interest of Money," Freud disciple Sandor Ferenczi says children transfer their fascination with the products of their body first to mud, then to sand and molding putty, then to stones, then to glass marbles, buttons, and the like. Before long, the children's original interest in dirty things is transferred to shining pieces of money, which are, according to the author, "nothing other than odourless, dehydrated filth that has been made to shine." By extension, says Ferenczi, the adult's interest in money is displaced beyond coins themselves to "all sorts of things that in any way signify value or possession." Paper money, checkbooks, credit cards would all clearly qualify.

Yet the foregoing is only part of the answer. The remaining and—as regards our money attitudes—perhaps even more significant part is this: Humankind has striven to distance money from its tangible origins because the id continually strives to divorce money from the *reality principle,* which compels us to employ our ego to function appropriately and responsibly in the civilized world. We wish to link it instead with the *pleasure principle,* which compels us to seek the removal of all obstacles to feeling good. The abstraction of money, in short, helps us to behave less responsibly and more impulsively.

French historian Fernand Braudel has written that "any society based on an ancient structure which opens its doors to money sooner or later loses its acquired equilibria and liberates forces which can never afterwards be adequately controlled. The new form of interchange disturbs the old order. . . . Every society has to turn over a new leaf under the impact."

Alas, the leaf modern man has turned over in response to contemporary forms of interchange has yielded some alarming consequences. For when the pleasure principle prevails with regard to money, two dangerously self-defeating attitudes toward it may result.

The first is: "I don't know."

The second is: "I don't care."

THE "I DON'T KNOW" ATTITUDE

Mr. G. pays for nearly everything by credit card or check. If he needs cash for small transactions like buying a magazine or a candy bar, he visits an automated teller machine located in the lobby of his office. He inserts a bank card that allows him to access his personal checking account, keys in an identification code, and punches up an "Amount Desired." Along with the money that the machine offers up in obedience to Mr. G.'s demands, a transaction receipt is proffered. But Mr. G. promptly crumples up the receipt and tosses it in a trash container. He never enters these transactions in his checkbook, even though he visits the automated teller several times a week. For that matter, he never enters the checks he writes in his checkbook register either.

But Mr. G. isn't concerned. Since his paycheck is electronically deposited into his checking account each week and since Mr. G. also has a large overdraft checking line of credit, the teller machine has never yet refused any of his requests, and his checks have never bounced. He has never been refused credit card approval either. Even though his payments are often late, he earns a very respectable salary, and his credit card companies keep upping his spending limits.

Though he never exactly knows if he's in the

red or in the black at any given moment, Mr. G. is confident that everything will ultimately work out. Life's too short, he says, and he can't be bothered worrying about money matters. Why, he hasn't even gotten around to filing last year's tax return yet.

Mr. G. obviously scores fairly high up there on the money-madness spectrum, but his mind-set is not entirely unfamiliar, even to those whose symptoms are not so pronounced. Many of us forget, at least every now and again, to make note of the furtive exchanges we have with money machines in the vestibules and parking lots of our local bank branches. Many of us miss payment deadlines, procrastinating endlessly in the face of financial paperwork. Many of us read the backs of cereal boxes more attentively than we read our bank statements.

Many of us, in short, try to avoid at least some of the nuts-and-bolts requirements of realistic money management as much as possible. It's too overwhelming, we say, or too boring, or just too damned hard. Most of all, we say, it's all too confusing. And, of course, we are right. Money matters *are* confusing, and more intangible and unreal the mechanisms of money get, the more confounding financial life can be.

Voluminous statements reflecting our pension and insurance plans read like hieroglyphics. It sometimes seems as if it would be simpler to compute the rate at which the universe is expanding than it is to compute how much money is in our Keogh funds. Investment choices are more baffling than ever.*
On the floor of the New York Stock Exchange, we can deal in *futures* or *options*. If currency trading is more our style, we can busy ourselves with *buying puts* or *selling calls*. If commodities are our choice, we certainly won't be dealing with bushels of actual corn and soybeans. We'll be betting on their future

---

* Documentation of investments is also more abstractly represented than in the past. Years ago, investors got ornately inscribed stock certificates and bonds with detachable payment coupons. Today, they get computerized records of their portfolio transactions.

prices or buying *indexes*, which allow us to bet on the ups and downs of the entire commodities market.

Even those who never put their money in anything more complicated than a wall safe cannot altogether escape financial befuddlement and anxiety—at least not if they file annual tax returns. Ostensibly, a plethora of help is available to mitigate the terror factor inherent in April 15, but the mere sight of a bookstore shelf full of 500-page guides to "simplified" tax codes can, for many, be cause enough to break out in hives.

Turning for help to the IRS itself offers precious little guarantee of auditproof accuracy. Shortly after the widely touted Tax Reform Act of 1986—which the U.S. Office of Management and Budget estimates causes taxpayers to spend an addition *105 million hours a year on paperwork—Money* magazine reported that IRS phone assisters offered incorrect answers to tax questions 41 percent of the time. Hey, if *they* don't know, we think, how are we supposed to know?

Just what *are* we supposed to know about our financial lives anyhow?

A *Forbes* article entitled "Watch Your Assets" distinguished between financial saints and sinners by defining the former as anyone who could answer—and answer quickly—the following questions: "What is your net worth? What income can you expect when you retire? How much would your spouse and family receive if you died? How much do you pay in taxes annually? What do you spend the most on every year? How much will it cost to send your kids through college and how will you pay for it?"

Needless to say, the vast majority of us fall into the sinner category. We don't know the answers to all these questions. What's more, in many instances *we don't really want to know.* Suppose we discover unpleasant truths? Suppose we can't reconcile the bottom-line numbers with our sense of *who we are?* Then our fantasy of having a financial security blanket to cling to may evaporate and we will be left feeling helpless, confused, vulnerable, and afraid.

Suppose we discover we are not in control of our financial

destinies as much as we'd hoped we were? That inflation has eaten away at our precious savings? That our holdings are insufficient to protect us and our families? Then we might feel shame and guilt, those "filthy" money feelings. Many of us would rather "wash our hands" of that dirty old thing called money and its newfangled complications than endure the frustrations of a hands-on approach.

The more convoluted modern money techniques and technology become, the more we feel justified in avoiding money management and its attendant responsibilities. Money's intangibility assists us in throwing up our hands and asserting we "have no head" for money.

But it serves another purpose as well. It has provided us with easier and easier ways of getting *over* our heads in debt.

THE "I DON'T CARE" ATTITUDE

Mr. H., forty-three, has filed for bankruptcy three times and candidly admits he plans to do so again. His financial strategy is simple: Every seven years he arranges to have his debts legally absolved. He then takes a job for a brief period of time and applies for new credit cards using a slightly altered version of his real name. When he has a pocketful of cards—which he terms "funny money"—at his command, he quits his job and travels around the world.

Mr. H. has become so adept at beating the system, and so knowledgeable about the ins and outs of finance and of bankruptcy law, that his friends have suggested to him that he ought to "go straight" and consider a career that would put his shrewd mind to constructive use. Investment banking, perhaps. They warn him that his shenanigans will one day catch up with him.

But Mr. H. points out that nothing particularly

unpleasant has befallen him yet. He insists that he is perfectly happy with his life-style and his "funny money" and declares that there is no shame in going bankrupt. "Even the Bible," he says, "mentions the release from debt every seven years."

Mr. and Mrs. J. are both employed. Together they have a household income that in their hometown of Columbus, Ohio, should allow them and their two children to live comfortably, without incurring any debt aside from a mortgage. But the J.'s found that when the first of the month rolled around, they were writing checks to fourteen different credit card companies. They had used the cards to purchase everything from the latest home video gadgetry to expensive antiques to closets full of designer clothing for themselves and their daughters. They even used several of the line-of-credit checks that came along with the cards to make a down payment on a built-in swimming pool.

Mr. and Mrs. J. say the fact that they were getting financially overextended did not bother them, because they always assumed they would "catch up." The only thing that was becoming a nuisance, to their minds, was the amount of paperwork they had to do each month to pay all their bills. In order to alleviate this problem, they went to a financing company that consolidated their debts into one monthly payment. Though Mr. and Mrs. J. say they are not certain exactly how long they will have to keep making this payment, nor whether the consolidation process is costing them more money in the long run, they are grateful to the finance company for removing the small frustration that stood in the way of their immediate gratification. Now that they don't have to write as many checks or lick as many stamps, they see no reason to curtail their spending. "We have everything we want," they reason, "and we have it now."

Nietzsche defined man as "the animal that can promise." That is because man can remember the past and imagine the future. Since we have always been able to promise, debt and credit of sorts have long existed. Long before the introduction of money per se, humankind has understood and employed the concepts "to owe" and "to pay." You give me something now, we said, and I'll make it up to you later. But as modern forms of money evolved, the promise implicit in debting was less frequently honored.

Coinage helped give overdebting a boost. It was also not long after standardized money's debut in Greece that debt default became widespread. Suddenly, if someone did not feel that he had enough of what he required or desired, he might be able to avail himself of the bright shiny discs that provided him with more in a relatively painless fashion. He usually fully understood only later on that the more he borrowed the harder it was to pay back what he owed. By that time, he might well find that discharging his debt meant being sold, or having members of his family sold, into slavery.

But if coinage gave debting a boost, modern credit instruments have given it a full-blown shove. We have charge cards in our pockets, overdraft checks in our desk drawers, and the whole of modern money technology at our side. We have *deferred payments* and *installment sales credit* (the kind used to buy refrigerators and furniture). We have *installment cash credit* (direct loans for personal purposes, like home improvements), *simple lump sum credit, open-end* or *revolving credit,* and all manner of special credit union plans.

Banks and savings and loan organizations offer us home equity loans that let us remortgage our houses and go on dream vacations. Brokerage firms offer margin accounts that let us borrow against the value of securities. Department stores up our credit limits at holiday time to allow us to purchase ever more extravagant gifts.

Credit card solicitations arrive in our mailboxes daily. It's not uncommon to arrive home after a hard day's work to learn that we have been "preapproved" for an instant credit line in the amount of thousands of dollars—a loan that years ago would have taken weeks to process. More than 10,000 types of credit cards are issued yearly in the United States alone. The average U.S. citizen totes more than three, but there's no telling how many of them each of us could get if we really applied ourselves to the task.

Walter Cavanagh of Santa Clara, California, ended up in the *Guinness Book of World Records* for having over a thousand credit cards issued in his name, and an average of four new ones arriving daily. Though Cavanagh's wallet weighs thirty-five pounds and contains $1.5 million in buying power, he only has approximately 12 percent of all the cards available to the general public.

Not surprisingly, overdebting has, for many, become a way of life. In the United States alone, where it has been estimated that the average American now spends 120 percent of his income, consumer debt more than doubled during the 1980s. Defaults on mortgages and auto loans stood at an all-time high by the end of the decade. Each year, credit card companies absorb billions of dollars in uncollected payments. Personal bankruptcies have more than tripled since 1970. On an average day, 1,500 Americans file for bankruptcy.

There are many reasons why one may allow his personal debting to get out of control, and each and every layer of the Money Complex can play a role in contributing to debting problems.

At the First Layer (The Intrapsychic Layer):

• We may overdebt because we choose to be defined by our acquisitions, buying things that boost our capacity for self-esteem or to try and fulfill a fantasy we have about ourselves. (The operative emotional association: Money is a security blanket.)

• We may overdebt out of an unconscious desire to impoverish ourselves, to get rid of our money because on some level we find it loathsome. (Money is filth.)

• We may overdebt because we feel unfulfilled and frustrated in some significant aspect of our lives and because spending temporarily takes our mind off our sense of emptiness and unhappy circumstances. (Money is food.)

At the Second Layer (The Family Training Layer):

• We may overdebt because compulsive behavior of one sort or another runs in our family—if not compulsive spending or gambling, then compulsive eating, drinking, or drug abuse.

• We may overdebt as a reaction against a family of origin where thriftiness was excessively prized.

• We may overdebt because we like to buy things for our parents, siblings, children, and partners in the hopes that they will give us the love we crave.

At the Third Layer (The Social Training Layer):

• We may overdebt to try to keep up with our peers, or with those whom we imagine we would like to have as peers.

• We may overdebt because we are unable to resist media messages which instruct us to "shop till we drop."

• We may even overdebt as an expression of attitudes of angst and pessimism that permeate the culture, reasoning that if we may all get blown up in a few years or, more likely, fry under an ozoneless sky, we may as well borrow as much as we can.

With all these inducements, clearly we cannot pin the sole blame for overdebting on the existence of credit cards and home-equity loans. Indeed, easy availability of modern credit instruments has not so much given us new reasons to debt so much as it has provided us with new rationalizations for doing so. The stronger our underlying propensities to debt, the more we will employ those rationalizations.

There was a time when we tended to associate the concept of debt with the concept of obligation (the German word for debt, *Schuld*, is the same as the word for guilt). Now many of us seem not to experience an attitude of obligation. We embrace instead, as Mr. H. and Mr. and Mrs. J. do, an attitude that says, "I don't care!"

"Funny money," as our Mr. H. would say, fuels the "I don't care" attitude by reinforcing the pleasure principle. For one thing, it prolongs pleasure by making it easier to delay and defer—and thus deny—for longer periods of time the inevitability of debt repayment. It's possible—and for many all too tempting—to spend months, even years, playing musical credit cards. We can pay off one account with a line-of-credit check from another. We can make, and indeed are encouraged to make, small minimum monthly payments on bank cards rather than paying the balance in full.

If we read all the fine print in our credit agreements, we might be shocked to learn that paying off a $3,000 loan on a minimum-payment schedule could, in some cases, require over a decade of incremental payments totaling many times the original amount borrowed. But, hey, who wants to read the fine print? That clearly falls into the domain of the reality principle.

Modern credit instruments also help mitigate the obligation factor of debting by emotionally distancing a borrower from the source of his borrowed money. It's harder to feel responsible to faceless, anonymous creditors who advance credit lines through the mail than it is to an avuncular hometown banker who puts a personal stamp of approval on a loan application, shakes the borrower's hand, and says, "See you Friday at the Volunteer Fire Department ball." Someone like Mr. H. might feel less that there was "no shame in going bankrupt" if he had to look his creditors in the eye and explain his "it's in the Bible" rationale to them.

Finally, modern credit techniques feed into the pleasure principle by reinforcing the grandiose infantile attitude that instant gratification is something to which we are entitled. Mr. and Mrs. J. articulate clearly that they want what they want when they want it. If what they want cannot be obtained from within, they believe they need only summon up help from without. They insist they will "catch up" with their obligations, but have no reality-based plan for doing so. Rather than attempt to formulate a long-term plan, they solicit a Band-Aid solution from a finance company which will, for yet more cost, consolidate their debts.

The "I don't care" attitudes of Mr. H. and Mr. and Mrs. J. are certainly somewhat extreme. No doubt, aspects of the intrapsychic dynamics and family and social training predisposed them to appropriate modern money techniques in the ways they do. Nevertheless, an inordinate number of people embrace a degree of the "I don't care" attitude in relating to debting. And a little here and a little there adds up to a big picture that is increasingly alarming.

Never-ending news updates on debt of staggering magnitude abound. If we open a newspaper or magazine, we can read that in America corporate debt now exceeds the net worth of all our corporations. We can read of the enormous debt undertaken by political candidates in the course of their campaigns. We can read of savings and loan bailouts and of economists who bandy about the idea of forgiving the Third World its debt of a trillion dollars.

Will someone bail *us* out of our credit card debts? Will someone forgive *us* the payments on our second mortgage? We can't help but hope so. After all, we meant no harm and, heck, even the *Vatican* is in debt for tens of millions. And so what if help is not forthcoming? Would that be the end of the world?

Some economists have come to conclude that the government budget deficits we hear so much about aren't necessarily so bad. Some don't even believe they exist. In January of 1989, when most experts agreed the deficit for fiscal 1988 was in the neighborhood of $155 billion, *The New York Times* reported that Robert Eisner, an economist at Northwestern University and former president of the American Economic Association, was contending, as he had for some time, that the U.S. budget was actually in the black. "Calculated his way," said the *Times*, "with special categories for things like capital spending and state and local budget surpluses, the Government accounts should show a handsome surplus of $42 billion."

All right!

It used to be a practice as well as a theory that one could compute one's financial net worth by deducting what one owed from what one owned. But modern money arithmetic seems to make use of different accounting methods. I once read a *Business Week* article on Japanese real estate mogul Harunori Takahashi, dubbed "the world's busiest man." The article informed readers that Takahashi "controls a diverse $7 billion empire," which includes resort hotels, electronics companies, portions of financial institutions, and prime downtown properties in Tokyo, Osaka, Hong Kong, Sydney, and Los Angeles. It also informed them that this enterprising gentleman's liabilities *also* totaled $7 billion.

Seven billion minus seven billion. There was a time when that would have added up to zero. But that time is apparently gone.

Mighty corporations, governments, and "billionaires" are burdened with debt. "The Donald" goes into the red and is put on a creditor-imposing budget of $450,000. A month. Who can blame us if we let our own mini-mountain of debts pile higher? After all, they are nothing compared to the Everest of debt that looms on the horizon. The numbers are too much to assimilate. It's too incongruous. Just too far out. Too unreal.

. . . .

As small children, many of us played a game where we placed a nickel, dime, or quarter beneath a blank sheet of paper and, by rubbing the side of a pencil point across the paper, reproduced the coin's markings on its surface. Poof, we had "made" money on the spot. As we grew up, we put this particular game aside, but we never renounced the fantasy that allowed us to enjoy it so much in the first place. At one time or another we have imagined how nice it would be if we could just conjure up some money.

The techniques and technology of money that we have created keep us playing such money games in adult life. They enable us to cling to the fantasy that more money can always be created as needed—without unhappy side effects. They help us have faith in money magic, and that, as we shall see in the next chapter, we are most inclined to do—not just individually but, quite literally, in droves.

6

. . . .

Pack-Think

. . . .

There is nothing more difficult to take in hand, more peril-
ous to conduct, or more uncertain in its success, than to take
the lead in the introduction of a new order of things.

—MACHIAVELLI
THE PRINCE

Think big. Think positive. Never show any sign of weakness.
Always go for the throat. Buy low, sell high. Fear, that's the
other guy's problem.

—DAN AYKROYD AS LOUIS
WINTHROP, IN *TRADING PLACES*

JOHANN SCHILLER, eighteenth-century German playwright,
essayist, and historian, posited that "anyone taken as an individual is tolerably sensible and reasonable—as a member of a
crowd he becomes a blockhead." As we already know, however, individuals are generally *less* than sensible and reasonable where money is concerned. Just imagine the possibilities
when they band together. For that is what the Fifth Layer of the
Money Complex entails.

THE TULIP TRAP

In the mid-sixteenth century, the tulip, long popular in Con-
stantinople, was introduced into Western Europe. The upper
classes of Holland developed an affinity for the fragile blossoms

and began importing quantities of them at extravagant prices. By the early seventeenth century, tulips had gained enormous cachet, and by the 1630s, as nineteenth-century British barrister Charles Mackay wrote in *Extraordinary Popular Delusions and the Madness of Crowds*, "it was deemed a proof of bad taste in any man of fortune to be without a collection of them."

Tulipomania, as Mackay termed it, soon made its way into the middle classes, and before long "people of all grades converted their property into cash and invested it in flowers." Bulbs of certain highly prized species sold for as much as 5,000 florins apiece—an astonishing sum, considering that with ten florins one could purchase, say, a nice chubby sheep or close to a hundred pounds of cheese.

The rage for tulips was so widespread, it was assumed that every Dutchman was well aware of it. Alas, there was one exception. Legend has it that a sailor who had been at sea during the height of the mania one day eyed a valuable bulb lying on the counter of a trader along with swatches of silk and velvet. Mistaking the bulb for an onion, he decided to eat it with his breakfast herring. When he was found down at the docks swallowing the last of the bulb—the cash value of which would have fed his ship's entire crew for a year—the unfortunate young man was sent to jail on a felony charge.

Ultimately, the sailor was not the only one to suffer from the effects of tulipomania. At a certain point, the realization began to dawn on the masses that the tulip rage could not last forever. The rich no longer had any interest in gazing at tulips but only in speculating in them. So where was the market now? The conviction spread that things would take a turn for the worse. Confidence fell, and so did prices. As the boom became a bust, pandemonium reigned among the dealers, merchants were reduced to poverty, and, as Mackay tells it, "many a representative of a noble line saw the fortunes of his house ruined beyond redemption."

The evolution of the tulip bulb from a trendy collector's item to a focal point for unbridled money hunger to an instrument of financial ruination (and thus once more a "worthless" plant root doomed to lie in the dirt) could hardly have been managed by any one individual in a state of isolation. Its rise and fall was a product of "pack-think"—the phenomenon that occurs when individuals surrender to the powerful primal impulse to merge themselves into a psychological mass.

Pack-think is the final layer of the Money Complex, but it is certainly a significant one. Even those who may envision themselves as rugged individualists cannot help but be at least subtly influenced by its force. And even if we were to understand every nuance of any given individual's money neuroses, we would still have to account for the fact that many individuals react differently—often far more precipitously—to money when they react as cogs in a collective wheel.

When it comes to money, as we have seen, we are influenced by various groups. Our money attitudes are at least partially formed in response to the messages of our family of origin, our economic class, our religion, and our national culture. But pack-think is not about groups. It is about crowds. And there are distinctive differences between the two entities.

Unlike a group per se, a crowd has no innate structure and shares no traditions or customs. A crowd is a relatively disorganized entity. It arises spontaneously. Yet it does have several characteristics that define it.

Members of a crowd generally have a common bond, often an interest in an object or goal (e.g., "Let's make a killing in tulips"). They share a high degree of reciprocal influence—indeed their thoughts and feelings might be described as contagious (e.g., "Tulips are swell" or "Tulips stink"). But, in addition, as the group theorist William McDougall summed it up, a simple unorganized group is "excessively emotional, impulsive, violent, fickle, inconsistent, irresolute and extreme in action, displaying only the coarser emotions and the less refined sentiments; extremely suggestible, careless in deliberation, hasty in judgement, incapable of any but the simpler and imperfect forms of reasoning, easily swayed and led, lacking in self-consciousness, devoid of self-respect and of sense of responsibility, and apt to be carried away by the consciousness of its own force."

Many who have studied packlike behavior would affix to this unflattering description a comparison of the behavior of crowds as entities with that of unruly children. Like an undisciplined child, a crowd as a whole tends to be heedless. Like a child, too, a crowd is credulous and weak in intellectual skills, such as those that lead to the ability to quantify and compare. (Before the age of six, children are incapable of representational thinking. If they see an identical quantity of water being poured from a tall, narrow glass into a short, wide one, they will insist that the tall glass contains more liquid.)

Like a very young child—or like an adult who is childishly adhering strictly to the pleasure principle—a crowd is poorly equipped to successfully restrain its unconscious id forces. It knows only that it wants to be fed when hungry, that it wants to be soothed when frightened. And like a child, a crowd is often given to "magical thinking"—a belief that wishing will make things so.

But here is a great irony: When a crowd has making money on its collective mind, for a time wishing *can* make things so. Physical reality is one thing (the aforementioned quantity of water remains the same regardless of the shape of its vessel) but social reality is quite another. As history has shown again and again, if enough people *think* something is true, it can *be* true—for a while.

In France in the early eighteenth century, the temporary creation of financial "truth" by pack-think was evidenced in an episode that came to be known as the Mississippi Scheme. In Paris, people went wild with glee at the opportunity to buy shares in a company established to trade in Louisiana and on the Mississippi River. The company was the brainchild of one John Law, a Scottish banker-cum-financial-savior who had infused new breath into the French economy by convincing the Duke of Orléans, reigning regent, to print paper money—and lots of it. At first, men and women of every age and social class clamored in the streets to buy shares in the enterprise of the man they worshipped. Values of the shares increased daily, sometimes rising 10 to 20 percent in a matter of hours.

Soon, however, things began to turn around. Beginning with a refusal by Law to redeem the shares of one stockholder, mass confidence began to falter. Before long, the man who had been a national hero was the butt of obscene jokes, ribald songs, and garish caricatures. John Law could venture forth into the streets only incognito or with a large escort and ultimately was compelled to flee to Venice. But France would never forget Law's moment in the sun—the moment when everybody believed he was infallible, and so he was.

In England at around the same time, similar pack-think dynamics brought on a similar scenario. In what came to be remembered as the great South Sea Bubble, crowds flocked to purchase shares in the South Sea Company, a venture which promised to exploit the resources of the South Seas and South America, blithely ignoring the fact that Spain had colonized the continent and was loath to grant rights of free trade. Not shockingly, the bubble burst, but before it did, South Sea shares rose fast and furiously, creating wealth out of thin air or, more accurately, creating wealth out of a powerful group wish to create wealth.

The recent past is also filled with stories of scams and schemes that enticed any number of people one might have hoped would know better into investing in everything from chinchilla ranches to earthworm farms (earthworms being, their promoters claimed, essential ingredients in products ranging from dog food to shampoo). Though the masterminds behind such financial fads often ended up in the slammer, the truth is that for a certain period among a certain group of people chinchillas and earthworms were what tulips had been in another time and place—money equivalents transformed by pack-think from the ridiculous to the sublime.

FAITH, BICYCLES, AND THE
VALLEY OF PLENTY

In a book called *The Crowd: A Study of the Popular Mind*, author Gustave LeBon noted that when psychologically bound groups form, it is as if individual cells have combined to form a new organism. The new organism can do what the cells in and of themselves cannot. One of the things the pack can do that none of us can do alone is to generate enough faith to fuel an economy.

We value money. But money is only money because a large enough group values it as such. Once it no longer does, all hell can break loose. Whether in Revolutionary America (where George Washington complained bitterly that "a wagon-load of money will scarcely buy a wagon-load of provisions"); in Germany between the wars (where it was cheaper to burn currency for fuel than it was to burn firewood); or in Brazil in the early 1960s (when, in the grips of prodigious inflation, parents urged youngsters not to save but rather to go out and buy something quick), when crowds lose confidence in money, "normal life" is no longer the norm.

That money is a matter of mass faith is exemplified by what happened in Canada's Comox Valley, a rural area about five hours outside of the city of Vancouver. Though Comox Valley translates as "Valley of Plenty," and though fertile farmlands and woodlands abound, the region developed largely as a bedroom community for the timber industry and a support community for a military defense base. In the early 1980s, when the military pulled a squadron out of the base, reducing the local population by 400 families, and when a dwindling demand for newsprint flattened the local timber market, the Comox Valley was plunged into hard economic times. That's when a brainstorm hit Michael Linton, a valley resident who had, in the course of pursuing his MBA, been struck by what he termed "the futility and absurdity of the conventional economic process."

Though there was still a supply of goods and services and

still a demand for them, Linton observed, there was, thanks to an 18 percent unemployment rate, very little money with which to pay for them. So Linton founded something called the Local Employment and Training System (LETS) and set out to create a local currency with which community residents could purchase goods and services from one another.

The LETS currency, called Greendollars, consisted of credits that could be spent as cash at any business establishment in the community (restaurants, groceries, hardware stores, etc.) or used as payment to any provider of services (doctors, dentists, lawyers) that agreed to participate in LETS. In other words, if a local resident had some shelves built in his living room and paid the carpenter in Greendollars, the carpenter could go out to dinner that night and use Greendollars to purchase his steak. The restaurateur, in turn, could use the Greendollar payments of his patrons to have new tires put on his car by a local mechanic, have his hair cut by a local barber, have his trees pruned by a local gardener, or perhaps have the local sign painter make a sign for his restaurant window reading GREENDOLLARS ACCEPTED HERE. If he wished, he could simply add his nightly total of Greendollars to his existing computerized account and save them up for whenever he needed them—just as one can do with conventional currency.

The most difficult part of establishing a local money, Linton told me, was "getting people to have faith." It took months and months to convince reluctant valley dwellers to give the LETS system a try. Ultimately, he helped them overcome their skepticism, partly by instructing them in its fundamentals by creating a simulation Monopoly-type game called LETS Play, and partly by convincing them—as matters got worse and worse—that they really had nothing to lose.

Linton compared getting people to have faith in a new currency to teaching people to ride a bicycle when they've never seen a bicycle before. "They might get on one, ride twenty feet, fall off and conclude that bicycles don't work. If you had thousands of people riding bicycles already, that would be an illogical conclusion. But if your bicycle is the first one on the block, you'd have every reason to be dubious."

Once Linton got enough of a crowd "riding their bicycles," more and more people joined the LETS network. For about two years the system, and thus the community, thrived. Over a quarter of a million Greendollars (each having the equivalent worth of one goverment-issued Canadian dollar) changed hands—or, to be precise, changed accounts. But then there was a confidence crisis. Some of the valley's large retailers pulled out of the system and some of the professionals pulled out as well. The dentist left town to fulfill a dream of operating a traveling clinic.

In the Valley of Plenty, people fell off their bicycles en masse. Pack-think brought a brilliant experiment to a crashing halt, illustrating that for all its innovativeness this unconventional economic process was subject to many of the same absurdities as any conventional one.

When I last spoke with Michael Linton, he was still avidly promoting LETS systems throughout British Columbia. But he is well aware that no matter how strong his personal faith in Greendollars, that faith will prove useless unless he can also induce it in a sizable group. For one or for even a few individuals to try to use a currency after it has lost credibility with the masses would be ludicrous. Imagine the reaction one might get if one insisted, for example, on paying for one's lunch in Confederate dollars. No matter how fervently the diner wishes his notes were acceptable tender, his individual wish lacks the potency of the wish of a crowd.

Just as mass faith is required to make currencies, it is also required to make markets—markets in virtually anything. As Lewis Lapham wrote in *Money and Class in America*, "Value is determined not by anything extraneous to human beings but by their desires." If a large enough crowd desires and decrees that pickled pig's lips should have significant monetary value, they will *have* significant monetary value—and, it should almost go without saying, engender the same kind of irrational and neurotic behavior associated with money per se—for as long as the crowd believes in its own proclamation.

With faith on the rise, everyone in possession of pickled pig's lips stands to gain. And praise for pickled pig's lips will be heard far and wide. "What delectable delicacies!" people will say. "They taste good and they're good for you." "I've heard they give you energy!" "I've heard they're an aphrodisiac!"

Once faith begins to falter, however, value can vanish with alarming speed. And those poor fellows *still* in possession of pickled pig's lips stand not only to lose big but to look and feel foolish. For here is another consequence of pack-think: Once commodities that were valued by the crowd fall out of favor, those commodities may, at least for a time, be disparaged, disdained, and treated like "filth."

"Pig's lips? I've heard they give you cancer." "Pig's lips? I heard they turn straight to fat." "Pig's lips. You can keep 'em."

Certainly it can be argued that of the huge numbers of people who purchased pig's lips some did so because they genuinely found them pleasing. To those aficionados, pig's lips have inherent worth simply because they are what they are. But such people will doubtless find themselves in a minority, just as people who buy, say, art for art's sake have in recent years comprised a minority.

Caught up in the Pac-Man-like getting-and-spending money-as-food frenzy of the 1980s, we as a society moved from individuals valuing art for the emotional sustenance and aesthetic pleasure it provides to a crowd viewing artistic "goodies" through a translucent curtain of dollar signs. Those who could afford Impressionist masterpieces paid tens of millions for them; those who could not gobbled up prints, lithographs, and anything they were convinced was up-and-coming art, holding tight to their faith in its financial potential despite the warnings of experts that appreciation (monetary appreciation, that is, not art appreciation) was far from guaranteed.

Writing of art mania in *The New York Times* in 1989, art critic John Russell lambasted art auctions that consisted of "gladiatorial scenes that . . . have nothing to do with the appreciation of art, let alone the love of it." If there remained any doubt that fine art had become a commodities market, it was dispelled early in 1990. After it was revealed that Australian billionaire Alan Bond had arranged in advance to borrow half the purchase price of Van Gogh's *Irises* from Sotheby's auction house (he later sold the painting to the Getty Museum for an undisclosed sum), legislators began forming committees to investigate practices, prices, and disclosure rules in art-world sales. Where a bona fide market exists, someone somewhere is usually trying to regulate it—as the superego so often tries to reign in the id.

But attempts to regulate markets are often to no avail. Even attempts to slow them down may prove futile. As any mania progresses, crowds grow hungrier and hungrier for whatever the focal object of the mania is. Consequently, what objects are available move about faster and change hands more frequently. As those same objects—be they paintings or pig's lips or stocks or bonds—fall out of favor, speed is also deemed to be of the essence. What chance does prudence have to prevail once the upward or downward momentum begins? As most everyone knows: very little chance. Prudence pales next to the zeal of the purchase-happy, just as it pales beside the wide-eyed horror of panicked sellers.

FEAR, GREED, AND CHAOS

In the wake of 1987's Black Monday, *The New York Times* asked John J. Phelan, Jr., chairman of the New York Stock Exchange, what caused the market to plunge. Phelan's reply: "Psychology was the most important thing." About ten days later, Ted Koppel, seeking to shed light upon the ups and downs of the stock market in general, asked Dr. Jay Rohrlich, a Cornell University psychiatry professor with a private practice on Wall Street, how many people are motivated to buy a stock more out of greed or fear than out of an intellectual decision. Dr. Rohrlich's answer was "One hundred percent."

It is certainly no news that psychology has a pervasive impact upon the Dow. And it stands to reason that mass fear and greed—the pack's manifestations of intrapsychic "security blanket" and "food" metaphors—are key factors in determining what will become of the investments we make. What *is* surprising is that we so often manage to diminish or discount the impact of these emotional forces.

We like to think we invest for rational reasons—and that the people who control our pension plans and investment funds do the same. But more and more of those who make it their life's work to analyze the workings of the stock market are concluding that it is sometimes driven by forces that defy rational analysis. Suddenly "chaos theory," the product of a relatively new branch of mathematics that has shown how seemingly inconsequential events can trigger earth-shattering phenomena, is being applied not just to physical systems—where it helps explain why it is so difficult to predict the weather or the wave patterns in a pond—but also to the dynamics of human opinion formation as they relate to the stock market, a system notorious for suddenly defying the very trends and patterns it has created.

Robert Schiller, a Yale economist whom *The New York Times* described as "the most prominent advocate of the view that markets march to eccentric drummers" and as one who has "abandoned the traditional economist's faith in the consistency of human behavior," put it this way: "You would think enlightened people would not have firm opinions about where the market was headed. But they do, and it changes all the time."

As opinions go, so goes the market. As James Ramsey, a New York University professor and "chaos specialist," explained, "When no one knows what's going on, or rather everyone has a different opinion, it's like a bunch of atoms bouncing around in a bowl. You get a whole continuum, and prices tend to remain in a steady state." It's when opinions become more homogeneous and reactions more similar that the market is likely to become more turbulent. The whims of mass psychology take over. As confidence waxes and wanes, crowds come to be ruled by the desire to get more and get it fast or to get *out* fast and head for the proverbial hills.

In Mel Brooks's comic routine based on an interview with the "2,000-year-old man," Brooks asks the ancient sage what the principal mode of transportation was back in caveman days. The old man replies, "Fear." Over the millennia, not much has changed. Terror can be a highly effective people mover, and when it spreads through a crowd, mass flight is often the result.

The word "panic" refers to an emotional state once believed to have been induced by the Greek god Pan, god of wild animals and of shepherds and flocks. But panic takes place not only in the animal kingdom. It exists as a potent force in the human realm. In financial markets, once the fright trigger has been pulled, individual investors and professional traders, already subject to a constant level of free-floating anxiety poised to transform itself from feeling to action, are as capable as any herd of buffalo of participating in a stampede. The impulse is the same: Do something! Anything! At a certain point only motion can serve to stave off the feeling that the world may be coming to an end.

Under certain circumstances, most people are susceptible to fear. But when scores of articles penned in the aftermath of 1987's stock market crash compared the events of Black Monday to an economic "heart attack," the metaphor applied not to the heart of any one person but to the wildly pulsating heart of the crowd. As a single organism, the market tried to grapple with the sudden reality of imminent doom. With shock and disbelief, it simultaneously registered and denied reality, its players thinking, en masse, This isn't happening, this isn't happening. But it *was* happening. And because investors and traders were acting and reacting as a pack, the more frightened they became, the more fear gained momentum. The market spiraled downward until the peal of the day's closing bell.

Initial intense high-level stages of fear, of course, cannot be sustained indefinitely, and once the panic phase has passed, fear can have effects on the market other than mass selling and downward movements. A recent market disaster can, for a time, keep investors out of the game. Because just as an individual who survives a heart attack may adopt a more cautious life-style, eschewing cigarettes and steak-and-egg breakfasts, crowds of investors that survive market heart attacks may adopt a cautious stance as well. When markets are flat for long periods of time despite positive signs in the overall economy, one may be fairly certain that fear, albeit in one of its less dramatic forms—trepidation—is at work. Though the investors who sit out like to think they are anticipating the future, they are, in actuality, reacting to the recent past.

Fear may also be at work when an upward movement in the market is seen. As one money professional, a vice president with a major brokerage firm, explained it, "In the world of institutional finance, everyone is performance oriented. If a market move of any consequence starts to develop, brokers and money managers have a fear of how clients react if they're out of it. Not wanting to be left behind, they get on the bandwagon, and that's the way a market rally can begin."

While a market rally may evolve out of fear, at a certain point the impetus behind its climb makes a subtle shift from fear to fear's flip side: greed. The more investors become universally entranced by the allure of instant money, the more greed will grow stronger than fear, replacing it as the prime motivator behind market movements and drawing more and more individuals into a crowded investment arena. The greater the number of people committing their funds, the more competitiveness and envy enter into the picture. The nagging dread that someone, somewhere may own a hotter stock is a powerful incentive to keep sinking more of one's own funds into the market.

Like fear, greed has the potential to affect virtually everyone. (To quote Shearson Lehman Hutton executive John Spooner, author of the book *Sex and Money*, "There are no sophisticated investors, only greedy ones, who, outside their own businesses are easier marks than daddies at their daughters' lemonade stands.") Like fear, collective greed has a primordial animalistic component. (In *Bonfire of the Vanities*, Tom Wolfe employs as a kind of refrain the provocative image of writhing, sweating "well-educated young white men baying for money" in the trading room of a prestigious Wall Street firm.) Like fear, greed feeds on itself. The more money investors commit to their wish, the more they want to believe that their commitments are justified. The dynamic is the same as in recreational betting, where, as a University of Michigan study has shown, people leaving betting windows were more confident by far of their choices than those who had not yet placed bets.

But perhaps the most significant similarity between fear and greed is that the latter, like the former, is capable of inducing in large numbers of people the impulse to abandon common sense and reason. Individuals cannot tolerate cognitive dissonance; but, amazingly enough, when greed affects individuals *acting as a group*, it can induce an astonishing capacity for tolerating the simultaneous conscious acknowledgment of two contradictory ideas without paying heed to the inherent conflict between them. Though, for example, hard facts may point vividly to the fact that stocks are overpriced, highly experienced professional fund managers caught in the frenzy of a bull market can often be just as likely as novice investors to deny and defy reality. They may scramble to buy more in the belief that the market will continue to rise *despite* the fact that it really has no concrete reason to do so. (As the adage goes: "Never confuse brains with a bull market.")

In *Group Psychology and the Analysis of the Ego*, Freud noted that "groups have never thirsted after truth." Rather, he said, "they demand illusions and cannot do without them. They constantly give what is unreal precedence over what is real." When fear and greed take root in the group mind of a crowd, they can create illusions on a grand scale. Yet these very illusions can, in turn, lead to results that are quite substantive. In this day and age, they can create billions and billions in assets. They can create thousands upon thousands of new companies and new jobs and business opportunities. And—presto!—they can make them all disappear. Once the Janus-faced greed-and-fear machine is operative, illusion and substance, the unreal and the real, walk hand in hand. But one might also wonder about the forces that set the greed-and-fear juggernaut in motion in the first place. How do they begin? Are *they* real or unreal?

One of the terms generated by chaos-theory research that has already made its way into the vernacular is something called the *butterfly effect*. It refers to the intriguing notion that the beating of a butterfly's wings in, say, Hong Kong could create a hurricane over the Atlantic. When it comes to financial markets, one can see how a butterfly effect of sorts can instigate major vacillations. The "butterfly" that instigates pack-think may flap its wings for reasons that are, in part or in whole, imaginary.

Rumors and speculations may create a flap. A hint that the trade deficit may grow, that interest rates are destined to rise, or that oil prices may be driven up can cause not just a reaction but an overreaction, in some circumstances bringing a market to its knees.

A whiff of exciting possibilities surrounding new stock issues can cause a flap. Investors love a good story. Thus, a new company offering the tantalizing possibility of a breakthrough in cancer research or cold fusion may, at the right moment, offer an emotional thrill that induces mass forgetting of all such companies that proved poor investments in the past.

Sometimes an entire story isn't even necessary. Exciting words alone may do the trick. Jack Dreyfus of the Dreyfus Fund said back in 1960, "Take a nice little company that's been making shoelaces for 40 years and sells at a respectable six times earnings ratio. Change the name from Shoelaces, Inc. to Electronics and Silicon Furthburners. In today's market, the words 'electronics' and 'silicon' are worth 15 times earnings. However the real play comes from the word 'furthburners,' which no one understands. A word that no one understands entitles you to double your entire score." Though in the 1990s the buzzwords *silicon* and *electronics* have been replaced with phrases like *genetic engineering* and *biodegradable,* one might suspect that *furthburners* packs as big a wallop as ever.

Any individual the public deems credible and powerful— i.e., any hero—can create a flap, and various investment gurus have at one time or another created self-fulfilling prophecies by predicting bull or bear markets. The more successful someone is perceived as being, the more mass obedience he can command. As one media consultant said of Michael Milken in his heyday, "If Michael had said the word 'sawdust' all of Wall Street would have run out and bought timber futures." Even the fact that a given guru's long-term track record may be found sorely wanting will not keep him from becoming perceived, at least temporarily, as a kind of financial Moses. So long as a few correct predictions are widely remembered, he will be followed—until a more glamorous guru comes along.

Any sizable like-minded subgroup within a crowd can cause a flap. "Chartists," for example, are a subgroup of technical analysts who search for esoteric patterns in the stock market as a means of predicting where it will go next. While others might look at graphs and see simple peaks and valleys, chartists may see a "head and shoulders" pattern or "three peaks followed by a house." Whether chartists' prognostications are valid in their own right is a source of debate. What is unarguable is that chartists, like other subgroups who band together out of a desire to predict market variables, are quite capable of influencing the very variables they purport to predict. As one trader put it, "I don't believe in chartism, but I definitely believe in chartists. You have to pay attention to them because there are enough of them to make things happen. If they think stocks will be worth more when the moon is full, they will be."

As often as flaps are created by actual events, or by out-of-proportion reactions to actual events, there are also instances where flaps are the result of nothing more than the shadows of the group mind. A herd of zebra can be seen bunching up or scattering wildly when they see, hear, or smell something that bodes an actual threat to their safety, but they can also be set off and running by an imaginary bugaboo, by fear itself. When author Michael Lewis recalls his days as a bond salesman, he confesses, "I spent most of my working life inventing logical lies. . . . Most of the time when markets move, no one has any idea why. . . . It was the job of people like me to spin a plausible yarn. And it's amazing what people will believe."

SHAMANS, STARS, AND SUPERSTITIONS

Once pack-think takes over, it's impossible to say exactly what will happen, where it will all end. It's only natural that we don't relish the idea. It's discomforting to think that our money is subject to forces that on the one hand we participate in creating and at the same time are so utterly beyond our personal control.

As small children, when our feelings were out of control, we looked to our parents to restore our sense of equanimity. For they, as we saw it, were privy to the magical secrets of the workings of the world. As members of a childlike crowd, we look to anyone we imagine might be privy to the secrets of money magic to take control over the twists and turns of the market, as well as control over our own anxiety and dread.

In our quest for control, we pay rapt attention to those whose job it is to analyze financial markets, in hopes that they can neatly and logically sum up whatever has occurred. We rely on them to reassure us that there's a method to the madness. As John Allen Paulos, Temple University mathematics professor and author of the book *Innumeracy*, puts it, "Commentators always have a familiar cast of characters to which they can point to explain any rally or decline. There's always profit-taking or the federal deficit or something or other to account for a bearish turn, and improved corporate earnings or interest rates or whatever to account for a bullish one. Almost never does a commentator say that the market's activity for the day or even the week was a result of random fluctuations."

In our quest for control, we look to bankers and brokers to dream up new financial instruments—like *portfolio insurance,* which, at least in theory, gives one the chance to make a profit in stock index futures as individual stock prices fall—to minimize risk and hedge against loss. If the hedges fail to provide adequate protection or, worse, backfire and accelerate a decline, our response is to hunt for yet more inventive contrivances.

In our quest for control we look to all manner of shamans to light our path, viewing those shamans through a veil of fairy-tale imagery. As Jane Bryant Quinn, *Newsweek* contributing editor and financial columnist, has commented, "Everybody's always looking for the 'tooth fairy' to follow when it's time to make investments."

In his book *Money: Whence It Came, Where It Went,* John Kenneth Galbraith complains that "those who talk of money and teach about it and make their living by it gain prestige, esteem and pecuniary return, as does a doctor or a witch doctor, from cultivating the belief that they are in privileged association with the occult." In fact, in numerous cultures throughout the world, from Samoa to Haiti to Navaho Indian society and African Zulu society, people with wealth are regarded as witches or sorcerers. But it's difficult to say who bears more responsibility for perpetuating the mystical aura surrounding money professionals—them or everyone else.

A large part of the pack's reverence reserved for those who ponder money for a living springs from the attitude of awe that many people hold toward anyone who is in regular proximity to money, or its equivalents or its representational data. Advisers and financial gurus and other "leaders of the pack," however, do not seem to believe *themselves* infallible. Indeed, sometimes they too take magical thinking to extremes, even looking to the heavens for guidance. Cornelius Vanderbilt employed mediums to channel stock tips from departed financiers, and J. P. Morgan routinely consulted astrologers concerning the market.

Far from being a thing of the past, financial astrology is still very much with us. For a few hundred dollars a year, New York astrologer Arch Crawford provides subscribers with the *Crawford Perspectives* newsletter, which interprets the market vis-à-vis constellations and planetary alignments (the conjunction of Saturn, Uranus, and Neptune in Capricorn, for example, purportedly spells trouble for the Dow). Crawford, a former technical analyst for Merrill Lynch, says the stars now tell him "when to be cautious." More than a few people seem to desire such celestial warnings. Crawford also serves as a consultant to professional and semiprofessional money managers, to a Middle Eastern bank and a Swiss brokerage house.

Stars aside, there are all manner of other "signs" that packs and their leaders watch for in the hope that herein they may locate the keys that unlock market mysteries. Take the Hemline Theory. It says that as hemlines rise, so go stock prices. Then there's the Superbowl Theory. According to this, if a team from the old American League wins the big game in January, the stock market will fall. If any other team wins, the market will rise. There's a Grasshopper Theory, which says the scarcer the insects become, the more likely a bear market will be. At one time there was even a Billy Martin Theory, whose adherents noted that when the Yankees rehired the controversial manager, more often than not the Dow tumbled.

In *Sex and Money*, John Spooner writes, "All people in the money business are superstitious. One broker I know will never buy stock beginning with the letter *c*, another will never buy a computer company; one friend of mine who left the business to make cheese in Vermont would never buy a company whose home office was in Dallas." Wall Street is rife with age-old wisdoms that vast numbers of people take to heart, from the maxim "Never buy stock on a Friday" to "Sell before Rosh Hashanah and buy back at Yom Kippur." Regardless of how many people subscribe to a particular superstition, the dynamic is the same. Superstition is, at bottom, also part of the quest for control—specifically the control of anxiety. As Isaac Asimov once wrote in the *Skeptical Inquirer*, "Inspect every piece of pseudoscience and you will find a security blanket, a thumb to suck, a skirt to hold. What have we to offer in exchange? Uncertainty! Insecurity!"

BUYING HIGH, SELLING LOW

Clearly, we have a strong psychological desire to allay feelings of uncertainty and insecurity where our money is at stake. But if one were to ask most investors what their chief desire is, this is not the one they would cite. They would not say they desire to believe in magic. They would not say they desire to follow the leader. They would certainly not say they desired peace of mind at a price. Their desire, they would say loud and plain, is simply to make more money! Their desire, they would insist, is to buy low and sell high.

Alas, pack-think makes it psychologically unlikely that most people will do so. Most people are prone to buy near the top and sell near the bottom, and thus keep in step with the rest of the crowd.

If everyone we know is snapping up Bioengineering Associates Inc. stock at $50 a share, we want a piece of Bioengineering Associates Inc., too. Soon, BAI is up to $75 a share, and we think what a good deal we've made. But do we sell it? Probably not. We wait for it to go up some more. But what if it doesn't go up? What if the flapping of some distant butterfly's wings causes it to drop back to $50 a share, then to $40 and then to $20? Why it's simple: That's when we sell!

But if we were really capable of putting our buy-low, sell-high strategy into practice, we probably would have resisted hopping on the BAI bandwagon while stock was on the rise, and we would have been tickled pink to buy it as it plummeted.

It is those who do manage to distance themselves from the crowd that tend to profit. Over a century ago, when the Baron de Rothschild was asked how he made his money in the French stock market, he revealed this strategy: "When the streets of Paris are running with blood, I buy." The baron obviously had no trouble understanding the precept that if everybody wants to do one thing, enormous opportunity may exist for those who do the opposite. His adherence to that precept—not just in words but in actions—earned him a reputation as a highly successful investment "contrarian."

The contrarian method is still as viable as ever. How it works, at least ideally, is basically simple. If there was a formal Contrarian Code of Conduct, it might go something like this: Contrarians do not go along with the pack. Contrarians do not pay heed to gurus or star charts or hemlines. They do not invest out of infectious glee or flee markets in a state of panic. Contrarians do not believe that the trend is their friend. Contrarians know better than to stay too long at a party. Contrarians make investments based on what they believe is the intrinsic value of those investments (in the case of stocks they use the price divided by earnings as a guide). Contrarians hold on to their investments long enough for the pack to rediscover them. Contrarians *actually* buy near the bottom and sell near the top.

Though no investment strategy, including contrarianism, is foolproof, contrarians have been known to make a good bit of money over the long haul. Warren Buffet, the very wealthy and highly respected investor who says his favorite holding period is "forever," is, for example, a committed contrarian.

The obvious question, then, is why aren't more people contrarians? Why do the same people who flock to the department store that has reduced its prices on swimsuits and loafers flee the stock market when it has reduced prices on securities? The answer, like the answer to so many seeming money mysteries, has more to do with feelings than financial facts.

Most of us want a *feeling* of safety, and are inclined to believe that there is safety in numbers. The idea of going against the crowd—even a crowd of lemmings heading straight for the sea—makes us anxious and insecure.

Most of us want *feelings* of approval and acceptance. We

dread doing something different, even in order to make money, if it means going alone out on a limb. (Besides, if we lose on money on our own, we lack "a good excuse.")

Most of us want *feelings* of excitement (the flip—and equally potent—side of our desire for safety). Being swept up in a giddy crowd can feel thrilling. Plodding along solo, even with good solid investments in our pockets, can feel woefully dull.

In 1934, a man named Ben Graham authored what has become a classic investment textbook. "Adam Smith" explains one of his key tenets this way: "According to Graham, following the market is like having a manic-depressive partner. Sometimes Mr. Market becomes so giddy he will ignore all reality and offer you outrageous sums of money for your part of the business. When Mr. Market is manic, you should sell him your part. Sometimes Mr. Market falls into despair, seeing no end of problems, and he will offer you his share of the business at a discount that would be silly. So you buy it. In between you keep your bat on your shoulder."

This may sound simple, but of course it is not. It is immensely difficult not to get caught up in mass mania and depression. The first Four Layers of the Money Complex already predispose most of us to take financial action on the basis of unexamined feelings. It is immensely difficult to stand on the sidelines and let Mr. Market have his mood swings while remaining objective. Far easier to let the Fifth Layer of the Money Complex carry us along.

Buying low and selling high is not for the fainthearted. And no one will be able to pull it off 100 percent of the time. No one can say with certainty what will happen to financial markets in the future. The dynamics of crowds assure that such a feat is beyond any expert's ken, whether that expert be self-appointed or pack-anointed. Even J. P. Morgan with so many successes under his belt and so many star-gazing advisers on his payroll, could say only one thing with certainty when asked what the market would do. "It will fluctuate," he said. And indeed he was—and always will be—entirely correct.

What's more, not even the most resolute contrarian is

likely to remain immune to the powerful emotions that are bound up with pack-think in moments of keen drama. As David Dreman, money manager, *Forbes* columnist, and author of *Contrarian Investment Strategy*, put it, "You can research market crashes that occur over a hundred years, but you never really think you'll live through one. Then it's something entirely different. All your standards are shattered. When you see IBM trade at 95, down from 125 in the course of a day, it's outside your realm of experience. You can structure your framework so that emotions have limited play with your investments. But you can't keep them out totally."

Not long after 1987's market plunge, I received a letter from a mutual funds group in which I had placed a small bit of capital. It was a letter acknowledging that recent events had brought "a great deal of anxiety" but urging a calm approach. "The best advice we can suggest right now," it said, "is that you make your decisions based on reason, not emotion." We will not be able to do that all of the time. With effort, discipline, and a respect for facts over feelings, some of us may be able to do it some of the time.

But those who cannot resist the greed-and-fear bandwagon at all might consider one of the following two approaches to the investment game as an alternative to their usual modus operandi. The first, ascribed to Will Rogers, is "Don't gamble. Take all your savings and buy some good stock and hold it till it goes up. Then sell it. If it don't go up, don't buy it." The second, ascribed to that old sage Anonymous: "Buy high, sell low, then lie about it."

. . . .

Pack-think may be thought of as the icing on the cake of the Money Complex. It tops it off, but it does not stand alone. One's intrapsychic money metaphors, the family and social messages one has absorbed, and the attitudes one develops in response to money's modern mechanisms can all play a role in predisposing one to be more or less susceptible to lemminglike behavior.

It is hoped that the remainder of this book will serve to help each reader discover the way the Money Complex manifests itself in his own life and what he can do to repair a damaged relationship to money. It is a task we must accomplish not as cogs in a careening out-of-control wheel but as individuals. For as Charles Mackay wrote, "[Humans] go mad in herds, while they only recover their senses slowly, one by one."

3
PART

- - - - - - - - -

**The
Money Complex
at Work**

•

**The
Money Complex
in Love**

- - - - - - - - -

Outside-Money,
Inside-Money

•

THE MONEY COMPLEX
AT WORK

. . . .

Those who are of the opinion that money will do everything
may very well be expected to do everything for money.

—LORD HALIFAX

MONEY IS A TOOL FOR LIVING. There is simply no getting
on without it. Whatever the nature or degree of our Money
Complex may be, we must throughout our lives weigh our
desire for money against what we are willing to do for it. And
we must live out our answer every day.

One of the key choices we must make with regard to
money is whether we will get it from "outside" or from "inside." Will we seek to be "fed" money from outside sources?
Or will we seek to "produce" money by our own efforts?

BEG, BORROW, STEAL, OR GET LUCKY

One day a patient, Ms. K., arrived at my office
in a highly agitated state. She told me that a week
earlier she had, on her way to keep her appointment
with me, been approached on the street by a well-
dressed young man who'd told her a hard-luck story.
His car had been towed for a parking violation, he'd

said, and he was without his wallet, which he had inadvertently left in its glove compartment. He asked if he could trouble her for a few dollars in order to get home by subway, get his checkbook, make his way over to the lot where towed cars are impounded, and ransom his vehicle.

Ms. K. was sympathetic. Her own car had been towed once, and she was well aware of the monumental kink such an event can put in one's day. The detail about the wallet in the glove compartment seemed a bit odd. This gentleman seemed like someone who would have known better. But we all have our moments of absentmindedness, she reasoned. And minor calamities so often seem to occur in tandem. She shrugged off any traces of suspicion she felt and offered the young man a five-dollar bill and some friendly words of commiseration. She also waved off his offer to send her a check for the sum she'd given him.

This week, she said, on her way to see me once again and following the same route as before, the same young man had approached her. Evidently without recognizing Ms. K., he began recounting the identical tale of woe. Ms. K. became incensed. She began shouting at him indignantly. She reminded him that she had fallen for his ruse once and threatened to call the police. She asked him, more or less rhetorically, how he could possibly stoop to such loathsome behavior. Much to her surprise, he responded to her question with equanimity.

"What's all the fuss?" he said. "All I am doing is making unsecured loans from strangers."

Whatever we may think of the man who attempted to put one over on Ms. K. (for reasons we shall soon discover, most of us would hasten to declare that *we do not think much!*), the notion of receiving an unsecured loan from a stranger—the idea of receiving hats full of money, no strings attached—is the common stuff of many of our prevalent money fantasies.

From infancy on, we desire, and indeed require, sustenance from the outside. It is a powerful desire, and not one we are likely to relinquish, despite the process of maturation. On some level, most of us imagine that it would be very nice indeed to have life's necessities—in our culture, read *money*—dropped into our laps.

It is no coincidence that decades after his disappearance from the airwaves some people still remember Michael Anthony of "The Millionaire" bestowing his seven-figure surprises upon fortunate souls. Nor is it an accident that game shows continue to capture the unflagging attention of millions of TV viewers. What a vicarious thrill it is to see that "Wheel of Fortune" spin!

Indeed, the First Layer money-as-food metaphor is so widespread that it reflects itself and is reinforced by numerous Third Layer media messages.

Yet, Michael Anthony and Vanna White aside, we know that to actually acquire exogenous money, that is, money from external sources, generally requires some action on our part. Alas, it is usually the kind of action that is unacceptable to our superegos, which concern themselves with issues of ethics, and our egos, which concern themselves with making pragmatic adjustments to the world at large.

How can we attract "outside-money" to us? We can beg or borrow or steal. But such endeavors present problems both moral and practical.

Unlike the man in Ms. K.'s anecdote, whose superego voices are obviously drowned out by those of his id, most people fortunate enough not to be obliged to beg view it as the last resort of the desperately needy. For the act of pretending to be in true need of charity when one is not, we have another name: freeloading. Moreover, the "give" messages we have received from childhood on tell us that charity is for the *other guy*. To accept it when we are in anything less than dire straits wounds our pride.

158

Borrowed money presents another problem. Though today more than ever, attitudes bound up in money's technology, the Fourth Layer of the Money Complex, can help us delay repayment to faceless creditors for lengthy periods, most of us reach a certain point in debting where we cannot fail to hear a nagging whisper, however faint, in the back of our head that reminds us the piper must eventually be paid. That whisper, a product of parental and social "shoulds" and a grudging nod to the reality principle, serves to eliminate borrowed money from the category of *truly* string-free lucre.

As for stealing money, statistics on tax evasion, employee pilferage, unpaid parking tickets, expense account padding, and the like would seem to indicate that vast numbers of us allow our id a little dollop of criminal satisfaction now and again. For most people, however, only a little dollop will do.

The late Edmund Bergler, a psychiatrist, posited that every neurotic (and when it comes to money, who among us can claim to be entirely neurosis-free?) harbors an "elastic fraud corner" that allows him to "cut corners with respect to the usual moral requirements." But even if the superego fails to kick into high-gear scolding at the prospect of a wee self-invented loophole, even if it allows us to occasionally believe we are the exception to a particular rule, in the majority of people, most of the time, it sounds a violent alarm at the prospect of big-time crime.

If conscience isn't enough to dissuade the majority of us from a life of larceny, there is always the ego, seat of logic, to warn us that usually, sooner or later, criminals tend to get caught. Most of the people that our society deems it acceptable to punish by incarceration or by fine are people whose "elastic fraud corner" stretches too far.

Of course, another way to obtain exogenous money is simply to get lucky. We may actively court luck by gambling, putting some funds at risk in the hope of receiving a reward that far exceeds the risk.

A minority of those who gamble do so compulsively. Unlike the occasional "Sunday" gambler, they are so preoccupied with betting that the bulk of their mental energy is devoted to computing their chances, forming and re-forming prognostications, and crafting daydreams about what they will do if they win. A number of theories have been proposed as to the etiology of compulsive gambling. Some who have studied the phenomenon view it as a psychodynamic problem and contend that compulsive gamblers feel compelled to provoke "fights" with fate, fights of such a dramatic nature that the winner literally takes all. Other researchers view it as more of a biological problem, contending that compulsive gamblers secrete lower than normal amounts of brain chemicals that regulate thrill and excitement. The act of gambling tends to raise these chemicals to more comfortable levels, they say, and it has been suggested that certain people may become physically addicted to gambling the way they might to a drug that alters brain chemistry.

Whatever the root causes of compulsive gambling may be in any individual, one thing is certain. No truly compulsive gambler is capable of quitting while he is ahead. Assuredly, he will take one risk too many and end up a loser. Thus, instead of being a way to avail oneself of outside-money, compulsive gambling turns out to be a way of ensuring that one winds up without very much money at all. As Mario Puzo put it in his novel *Fools Die*, "The house has an infinity of nights, and every one of them with the edge, the percentage."

But what of the recreational gambler? What of the individual who spends a fraction of his discretionary resources at casino roulette tables, at racetracks, or in slot machines? What of the bingo player and the weekly purchaser of lottery tickets who responds to ads that tell him all he needs to have a shot at pots and pots of outside-money is "a dollar and a dream"?

The first lottery was concocted in Rome over 2,000 years ago, and games of chance have been an integral part of the recreational life of numerous cultures. But here and now, gambling has become ubiquitous, part of the weekly or even daily routine of millions. What is on our minds when we wager? Do we really imagine our bets will result in producing a life-transforming treasure at the end of the rainbow? Or are we just putting the reality principle on hold long enough to have a little fun?

In most instances, the latter would seem to be the case. To gamble recreationally is to take a break from the voice of reason and let the voice of fantasy temporarily hold sway.

Studies show that the vast majority of ordinary gamblers engage in some sort of magical thinking.

> They may, for a time, overlook the laws of probability in favor of "the gambler's fallacy," which, as John Allen Paulos explains it in *Innumeracy*, is "the mistaken belief that because a coin has come up heads several times in a row, it's more likely to come up tails on the next flip." (In reality a coin knows nothing about its previous behavior and may come up heads or tails at any time. The outcome of each flip is independent of the past.)

> They tend to recall their wins far more vividly than they recall their losses, and thus believe that another win will occur sooner rather than later.

> They may, for a while, apply the "If at first you don't succeed. . ." credo to games of chance, a realm in which it simply does not apply.

> They may cheerfully ignore the odds against them, even when those odds are astronomical, as they are, for example, in most state lotteries.

But for the average gambler, these types of faulty thinking last only so long and go only so far. They may sustain the pleasurable fantasy of easily obtained outside-money for a few hours, but they, too, eventually bend to the voice of reason. Most of us know deep down that while gambling may now and again bring a little outside-money our way, it's hardly likely to provide enough to keep a roof over our heads or send our children to college, let alone provide us with Lamborghinis and Baccarat and the other luxurious stuff of our most gluttonous pecuniary dreams.

But what if it did? What if we were the big winner of the Irish Sweepstakes or Super-Humongous-Big-Cash-Money Lotto? What if we didn't gamble or actively court luck at all but nevertheless came home one day to find Ed McMahon's avuncular visage staring at us from an envelope and informing us that this time—no kidding—we actually had won millions and millions, courtesy of a benevolent magazine publisher to whose publications we'd never even subscribed. Would we be delirious? Sure. Would our rapture last? Perhaps not. Perhaps we would be guilty, ashamed, and undeserving. Perhaps we would fear that "the gods" made a mistake and, upon realizing it, would visit some trouble upon us.

Perhaps we would find ourselves among the ranks of people that become deeply depressed after a monumental infusion of outside-money. Perhaps, like many big-money lottery winners, we would forgo the odysseys we once imagined great riches would enable us to embark upon and settle instead for a larger, higher-definition screen on which to watch reruns of "Gilligan's Island."

In the movie *The Color of Money*, pool hustler Fast Eddie Felson, played by Paul Newman, rhapsodizes, "Money won is twice as sweet as money earned." But the truth is, fantasies aside, most of us don't really think so. In America, a culture mightily influenced by Puritan tenets, it would seem that all outside-money, whether actively sought or passively received, whether "ill-gotten gains" or a legitimate windfall, has something of a stigma attached to it. In our culture, the social superego, imbued with the ethic of pulling oneself up by one's bootstraps, overwhelmingly shakes its head and clicks its tongue at the prospect of outside-money, which it equates with "easy money." It warns us against bowing to its temptations, lest we be utterly ruined. Easy come, easy go, after all.

In our culture, without question, the most heartily approved way to come by one's money is to earn it.

THE MONEY MOTIVE

Unlike the legendary goose that laid the golden egg, we cannot literally create money to come from out of our bodies. But we can do the next best thing. In order to obtain money, we can make a trade of sorts. We can swap our energy, the labors of our body and brain, for financial remuneration. In this sense, earned money may be thought of as inside-money, for, as our vernacular has it, earned money is money we "make."

But like the obtainment of outside-money, the obtainment of inside-money involves choices. Just what kind of work is each of us willing to do? How much of it are we willing to do? How far are we willing to go to satisfy our fiscal desires? What other work-related goals—if any—will take precedence over pecuniary ones?

It is simple enough to grasp the premise that money can be gained via metabolic effort. Even chimpanzees are adept at making the connection. In a 1936 experiment done at the Yale Primate Laboratories, chimps learned that in exchange for performing rudimentary tasks they would receive coins they could feed into a vending machine that dispensed grapes. Not surprisingly, the tasks were accomplished with alacrity. When coins were given out freely, however, the chimps abandoned their chores. One might assume that the chimps—who know not from superegos or ethics, Puritan or otherwise—had no qualms whatsoever about freeloading. One might also conclude from the rapidity with which they abandoned their labors that, for them, work was *strictly* about making money, nothing more.

For us, matters of work and remuneration may be infinitely more complicated. Then again, sadly, they may not. We humans by and large have options concerning the work we do. One of those options is to work purely out of a money motive. Like chimps, we may perceive our work as something we do for pay—an activity in which we might not otherwise have any interest. But when money is the only reward we get for our work, we may well feel impoverished in other crucial ways.

When Mr. L., thirty-four, was in college, he assumed he would be delighted one day to earn $20,000 a year. Upon graduation, he decided that $50,000 a year was more like it. Soon after beginning work as a Wall Street trader, he set his annual goal at ten times that. Though for the next several years he fell short of the half-million mark by several hundred thousand dollars, he vowed to keep at his occupation until he had "a home on Park Avenue and a yacht." Ultimately, however, he began to feel bored in his work. The job he'd once found endlessly fascinating had for him become enervating. Wondering if he might be approaching burnout, he confided in an old friend, who encouraged him to take a series of aptitude tests. Mr. L. took the tests, which indicated that he had interest and notable skill in the area of psychology.

"I wasn't surprised to hear I might make a good psychologist," Mr. L. said. "I have the quintessential trader's gift of figuring people out right away, and I've always been good at getting people to open up about themselves." While the idea of earning a psychology degree held great appeal for Mr. L., he decided that going back to school was out of the question. He went back to trading instead, explaining, "I just can't stop doing what I'm doing until I live up to my own financial expectations of myself."

Mr. M., forty, is a management consultant employed by a nationally known consulting firm. It is the sixth firm he has worked for since entering this line of work in his mid-twenties. Since he has been with his present employer for almost four years now, he is beginning to think it is time to move on again. The next time a headhunter calls him with a tempting prospect, as tends to happen with some regularity, he plans to investigate. He knows he will inevitably receive a larger salary increase by switching from his company to one of its competitors than he will if he stays put.

Mr. M. does not especially relish the thought of leaving his current job. He genuinely likes and admires many of his colleagues. He has an impressive office, an efficient assistant, and a short commute. He's built up some vacation time, too. And he laments that over the years his job-hopping has caused him to forfeit a number of pleasurable trips which his wife and children had happily anticipated. But, be all that as it may, he is planning to update his resumé. "If you stay too long in one place," he insists, "you're just asking to be taken advantage of. I see people all around me who are loyal and patient. They don't have much to show for it. If you want real money, you've got to stay in motion."

Ms. N., thirty-eight, left her corporate law firm five years ago to start her own law practice. She wanted to concentrate only on cases that interested her, and felt she was prepared to earn less money in order to do so. She knew this would not present any true financial hardship, particularly since her husband earned a handsome salary as a public relations executive. But once she was actually out on her own, her attitude changed. She felt continually anxious about her reduced income. "Soon it became a matter of pride to me," she says, "to prove I could make as much money by myself as I had before.

Then it became a matter of pride to prove I could outdo my former income."

Contrary to her plans, Ms. N. found herself taking on cases she once would have griped about and working with clients she disliked. Though she had rarely worked less than sixty or seventy hours a week when she was on the firm's payroll, she now works even more. Her time has become so tightly budgeted that taking a weekend off to go out of town to her best friend's wedding seemed like a monumental sacrifice. Though she did make the trip, she insists she had no time to pack. When she landed in the city where the wedding was taking place, she headed straight for a department store and bought two days' worth of clothing, from undergarments to a formal dress, and a complete supply of makeup. "It was expensive," she admits, "and I remember sitting through the ceremony calculating how many extra hours I would work to offset the loss. I can't really say I got into the spirit of the happy event."

Ideally, the work we do in adulthood can make significant contributions to our psychological, social, and spiritual well-being. If we let it, it can be a healing experience, even mitigating many of the emotional deficits of early childhood. Nelson Aldrich has properly deemed work "the world's best therapist." It can provide us with a feeling of pride, with a sense of purpose, with opportunities to transcend the self. At times, work can even be responsible for inducing in us a kind of euphoria, the state of "flow," as Dr. Míhaly Csikszentmihalyi has termed it, that results from complete absorption in an activity.

According to Csikszentmihalyi, professor of psychology and education at the University of Chicago, the exquisite feeling of flow occurs when one is both unselfconscious and alert and when thought grows effortlessly out of action—in short, when one is performing at one's peak ability. Flow can be achieved by anyone engaged in any activity that presents a challenge sufficiently suited to one's level of skill. If a challenge is too great, anxiety interferes; if, on the other hand, the challenge is easily mastered, boredom will forestall flow. A dancer in mid-leap, a painter in mid-stroke, a basketball player in mid-slam-dunk can all serve to exemplify the phenomenon, but people involved in a process they find absorbing, from the planting of corn to postindustrial tasks like the trading of bonds or the writing of advertising copy, can experience flow.

What determines whether or not flow takes place is not *what* is being done but *how* what is being done is approached. As those who study it note, flow is *not* likely to occur when the desire for rewards, such as money, outweighs one's intrinsic motivation. Flow involves the pursuit of activity first and foremost for its own sake.

The many positive things that work can provide, including flow, are, most of us would agree, among the things that make life worth living. But we are not so likely to avail ourselves of them when money comes first and what we do to get the money comes second. Still, many find it difficult to order their priorities in any other fashion.

Two attitudes engendered by the Money Complex make it difficult to relegate the money motive to second place when it comes to our work. The first is our tendency to identify ourselves with a sum of money; the second is our tendency to equate money and time.

WORK, PAY, AND TIME

To a large extent, as noted earlier, the tendency to identify ourselves with a monetary amount ties in with the security blanket metaphor that is part of the Money Complex's First Layer. Investing money with a quality of selfhood and employing it as a self-soothing agent, we may describe ourselves *to* ourselves at least partly in terms of our salary (as in "I am worth $40,000 a year") or, if our work is not remunerated by a salary per se, then perhaps by the amount of money we earn per deal executed, project completed, or client serviced (as in "I am worth $1,000 per jingle written or $500 per root canal performed"). In our culture, this sort of equation is reinforced by Third Layer social messages as well, serving to make it particularly powerful.

Even if one made an assiduous attempt, it would be hard to escape the barrage of information that routinely informs us who is earning how much. The salaries and bonuses of Fortune 500 executives appear regularly in business magazine cover stories. The yearly takes of Madonna and Michael Jackson are practically shouted from the rooftops by those who report on entertainment and finance. The staggering sums offered to Ronald Reagan on the "mashed-potato circuit" made the network news. Michael Milken's annual wages at the height of his junk-bond reign at Drexel Burnham Lambert (a mind-boggling $550 million, which, as the *Wall Street Journal* noted, is nearly $100 million more than Guyana's gross national product) were the stuff of headlines.

All of this reportage seems implicitly to invite us to compare ourselves with those who are in receipt of outrageous fortunes. On the face of things, we may accept with equanimity a rock and roll idol, an ex-president of the United States, or a corporate mogul making far more in the course of one concert, lecture stint, or successful leveraged buyout than we will earn in a year. We can even comfort ourselves with the fact that, in the penitent '90s, Michael Milken had to pay *more* than $550 million in fines. Yet, underneath, we may smart with the sting of feeling undervalued. To patch up our torn dignity, we may comfort ourselves with thoughts of increasing our income in the future. But if we see money as an end and work as a means, we will think of increasing our income by working harder and longer and faster—not by becoming more emotionally or intellectually engaged with our work or by enjoying work more.

. . . .

Just as the comparison of money and self contributes to our perception of work as a commodity, so does the comparison of time and money.

The link between time and money is one that is deeply ingrained in our psyches. We live in a temporal world as well as in a monetary one. But both money and time—at least in the sense of measured units, e.g., hours, minutes, weeks, and months—are our inventions. Being products of the human imagination, they are ideally suited to reflect the projections of that imagination. And both are so fundamentally overwhelming that as soon as we conceived of them we felt compelled to gain power over them.

Like money, time can be "wasted" and "spent," and it can also be "saved." The more we can save it, and keep it from "slipping through our fingers," the more we feel in charge of it.

From Karl Abraham on, those who have written on the dynamics of anality have noted that the same impulses that lead many of us to feel powerful by hoarding money and by keeping relentless track of it can lead us, too, to be overly concerned with time "management" and overly precise regarding time. What's more, just as those impulses may cause us to fear that others may be out to extract money from us, they may cause us to live in dread of someone encroaching upon our precious time. A truly withholding character might respond to the query "Do you have the time?" by suspiciously countering, "For *what*?"

On the other hand, many of us are prone to surrender our precious time willingly enough if we can swap it for money. So we may spend an inordinate portion of our lives doing work that will net us a profit.

The connection of time, money, and work is a natural outgrowth of the time-money equation. When we say, "Time is money," we are referring, of course, to units of labor time. Indeed, the first impulses to organize time grew out of commercial incentives. As Daniel J. Boorstin points out in *The*

Discoverers, "the very purpose of a calendar [was] a time scheme to hold people together, to ease the making of common plans, such as agreements on the planting of crops and the delivery of goods."

It should come as no surprise that references to both time and work appeared in tandem on the first national coin struck in America. On one side of the 1787 coin, whose design was commissioned by Congress, was a chain of thirteen links surrounding the motto "We Are One"; on the other side was a sundial, the noonday sun, and the word *fugio,* the three elements signifying the maxim "Time Flies." Below the dial was the phrase "Mind Your Business," an "admonition to diligence," says a Federal Reserve brochure on U.S. coins and currency, "in the spirit of Poor Richard."

Over the centuries, humankind has devised an astonishing number of inventions the goals of which are to save time via shortcuts and acceleration. Fast transportation, fax machines, and fast food help us shave ticks off the clock. Yet studies show *leisure* time is on the decline. In a 1988 nationwide survey conducted by the National Research Center of the Arts, Americans reported a median of leisure time of 16.6 hours a week, a decline of 9.6 hours over a previous fifteen years.

The time we save is spent not relaxing, but *earning.* A study done for the National Bureau of Economic Research shows that people are even inclined to sleep less when financial incentive is involved. When time on the job is perceived as more valuable, even dreams, apparently, are allowed to go by the boards.

Many of us feel guilty, restless, and uneasy when we spend our time at endeavors other than those which result in the making of money. As a result, we may become obsessed with work, even addicted to it. We are afraid to stop. Afraid to fail. Afraid of being left behind. Afraid of being have-nots. And perhaps afraid, most of all, of the thoughts and feelings we might have to face if we stopped filling up every moment with the drive to convert energy into material gain.

Should anyone point out that the expenditure of energy

and time on behalf of the money motive does not translate into pleasure or true self-esteem, the sort that derives from an unassailable belief in one's inherent value, we may protest that we simply do not have the time to worry about such matters.

But here's something that might make even the most relentlessly acquisitive among us slow down long enough to pay attention: Though work that is emotionally ungratifying may certainly prove lucrative, *the money motive is not necessarily the best way to make a lot of money.*

THE PARADOX OF MONEY INDIFFERENCE

If we really want to seek our fortune through labor and enterprise, i.e., from the inside out, we might well do better to abandon the question "What will I get *for* this work?" in favor of the question "What do I want *from* it?" If our answer genuinely turns out to be adventure, enlightenment, or simply amusement, chances are we are closer to reaping monetary rewards than we may know.

What many of the world's most renowned creative artists, inventors, scientists, and even industrialists have had in common is an obliviousness to money's addictive properties. (It was Andrew Carnegie who called the mere amassing of wealth "one of the worst species of idolatry.") Rather than putting their energy into money worship, they bring an enviable vitality to their endeavors, often inducing an infectious enthusiasm in those around them. Rather than viewing their work as a means to an end, they view it as never-ending and everintriguing. Even the dog-work between the high points, the stalls, and the agonizing dead ends before the breakthroughs, while hardly "fun" in the classical sense, are perceived as part of the compelling overall process.

For the outside observer, it can be difficult to discern the distinction between the lover of work and a compulsively money-motivated worker. Both may put in exceedingly long hours, both may be intensely preoccupied with the details of their endeavors, and both may appear to devote total focus to the work with which they are involved. But there are distinctions.

The highly money-motivated worker, despite his seeming occupational preoccupation, is often obsessed with accruing enough rewards for his work so that he may one day put an end to it. Ironically, the alleged goal of a great number of so-called workaholics is early retirement. A genuine work-lover wouldn't be even slightly tempted to stop working should all the riches in the world be deposited on his doorstep. Why should he? For him, work is, in the best sense, play.

The highly money-motivated worker tends to pursue conventional occupations, in particular those his contemporaries accept as being safe bets for producing impressive revenues. In the mid-1980s, for example, a money-motivated college graduate entering the workforce would have been more likely to pursue a job in investment banking than, say, in environmental research. A genuine work-lover is far more likely to make unconventional choices, to take risks, and to devote his efforts to endeavors that may, at their inception, be perceived by others as sheer folly (as was the "horseless carriage," for example).

The spontaneity of the highly money-motivated worker is undermined by tension. A genuine work-lover is more likely to make great creative strides.

The determination to pursue one's passion regardless of perceived obstacles, though not a stance assumed for its profitability, can nevertheless be extremely profitable. Like unpopular stocks, unpopular pursuits may pay off big. It may well turn out that someone who indeed began in the mid-1980s to address himself passionately to the problem of how to replenish the ozone layer or what to do with our garbage will one day, in addition to a sense of accomplishment, find himself the recipient of material rewards that are the stuff of bankers' dreams. What's more, instead of converting energy into dollars, the genuine work-lover can use his passion to generate more energy. The energy snowballs, and often enough along the way a certain amount of wealth is created, almost inadvertently.

Bill Gates, the genius behind Microsoft software, who had by his early thirties, according to *Fortune*, "made more money than anyone else his age, ever, in any business," admits to enjoying his wealth, partly because he can now afford "suitable clothes" and a cleaning lady, but says that dwelling on his assets is "stupid," and that he is far more interested in the contribution his company is making.

Sam Walton, the multibillionaire founder of Wal-Mart Stores, who lives in Bentonville, Arkansas, drives a pickup truck and tells his employees, "Just call me Mr. Sam," seems similarly underwhelmed by money's ability to dazzle. After losing a whopping $1.7 billion on 1987's Black Monday, he was widely quoted as saying, "It was paper when we started, and it is paper afterwards." When he was listed first on the Forbes 400 list of wealthy Americans, Walton cheerfully told the editors he could "kick their butts."

Such individuals, self-made successes whose "secret" seemed to be a prime concern for results rather than for revenues, offer a valuable lesson for us all. Though it may seem paradoxical that a degree of indifference to money can result in the accrual of money, it is a paradox well worth bearing in mind when contemplating one's career path.

To all this, however, there is another side of the proverbial coin. When it comes to the generation of inside-money, is there such a thing as *too much* indifference?

As an oft-told story about Albert Einstein has it, when the eminent physicist was offered a position at Princeton and told he could name his salary, he asked for $3,000 a year. It was a sum so ridiculously paltry, even for the 1940s, that the university more than quintupled it voluntarily. Happily, Einstein, who had his mind on cosmic matters, had others looking out for his welfare. Not everyone is so fortunate, and it may well be argued that while a certain benign indifference to money may turn out to be a financial blessing, such an attitude can, if taken to extremes for neurotic reasons, evolve into a self-induced curse.

There can be a fine line between a mind-set that allows us to master inside-money by transcending it and a mind-set that compels us to do ourselves in financially. But where exactly does this line lie, and how do we know when we've crossed it?

As we shall see, the line tends to get crossed when people harbor money attitudes that reflect and reinforce a sense of personal inadequacy or unworthiness.

THE ART OF SELF-SABOTAGE

Dr. P. and Dr. Q. have two things in common. Both always wanted to be doctors. Both always professed to have little interest in money. After college, Dr. P. attended medical school and following his residency decided to devote himself to research in neurology. Dr. Q. did not get into medical school. He was deeply disappointed, feeling he'd let himself and his whole family down. Nevertheless, he rallied and decided to go to veterinary school instead. He'd always adored animals, and it did not seem like a bad alternative.

Dr. P., having chosen a field of medicine that was not particularly lucrative, still maintained that money was not an issue for him. Indeed, for many years he was not nearly as well compensated as many of the other doctors with whom he'd graduated. But in time his research came to be recognized as highly important and innovative, and he received substantial grant funding. He was also offered numerous opportunities to teach and to lecture, and gained a reputation for being extremely skilled at imparting complicated concepts in a facile and entertaining way. Ultimately, he was contacted by a book publisher and asked to write a popular book on the human brain. He did, and it sold quite well. Now he is at work on another.

Though he is still not particularly concerned with money, Dr. P. seems to have made quite a bit of it. His "disinterest" in finances prompted him to put most of his funds in the hands of a money manager who came highly recommended by several other doctors. The choice of this money manager turned out to be a sound one. He compiled a profitable portfolio of diversified investments which would assure Dr. P. a very comfortable future. Once a year, Dr. P. reviews his portfolio with his financial adviser so that he knows where he stands. He dislikes these meetings, and grumbles and complains whenever their time comes, but he attends them anyhow. He says he'd like to make enough money to establish a scholarship fund for neurology students, "so I suppose I owe it to them to keep an eye on things."

Dr. Q. obtained his degree in veterinary medicine and opened a private practice. He found that he enjoyed his work and before long had a large and loyal following. Pet owners liked bringing their animals in to see Dr. Q. He was not only competent but had a soothing manner that seemed to put not only people but their cats and dogs at ease. What's more, he did not charge very much. In fact, his fees were far lower than those of other vets in his town—though no one could figure out why. Perhaps, his clients thought, he didn't need the money.

As it happened, Dr. Q. did need money. He had

large loans to pay off—though he was never quite
certain what his debts totaled—and was the sole
supporter of a wife and three children. In addition,
his overhead was high, and he was determined to
have the finest equipment for his office. He always
seemed to be struggling to get his income to match
his outgo. Yet he was always reluctant to raise his
rates. To everyone else, Dr. Q. said this was because
he cared so much for animals that he did not want
to contribute to making the cost of properly caring
for them prohibitive. To himself he mused that he
really was not worthy of "living the good life." His
failure to get into medical school had played upon
his longtime suspicion that he might be a failure all
around. He felt like a have-not and thought he
should consign himself to live as one.

The cases of Drs. P. and Q. exemplify the difference between benign detachment from money and financial self-
defeat. While Dr. P. is genuinely disinterested in the pursuit of
money for its own sake, he is not averse to reaping his just
rewards for work well done. Though he chooses to let someone
else deal with the nuts and bolts of his financial life, he has also
selected that someone wisely. And though he prefers to think
about the firing of the brain's synapses more than he does
about municipal bonds, he is willing to grit his teeth and set
his own brain to contemplating interest rates when necessary.

Dr. Q., however, while outwardly professing to have no
use for money, has a very distinct psychic use for it. He employs money to reinforce his negative self-image and to punish
himself. That is why, despite the talent, tenacity, and time
invested in his work, he can never seem to get out from behind
the financial eight ball. In this respect he is, unfortunately, far
from alone.

In recounting the stories of their lives in the course of
psychotherapy, each of the following four people revealed a

propensity for self-defeating monetary behavior. Later, as we shall see, they came to terms with some of the emotional conflicts underlying that behavior.

Mr. R., whose passion is computers, worked for many years as an editorial assistant on a personal computer magazine. It was well known throughout his office that he did most of his boss's work in addition to his own. He generated article ideas, rewrote and edited copy, selected graphics and photos, all with great skill. He never demanded any credit and was generally self-effacing. Because Mr. R.'s boss had personal connections high in the conglomerate that owned the magazine, letting him go was unthinkable. Finally, however, the boss retired, and Mr. R. was offered his position. He accepted the promotion, though the salary he was offered was a fraction of that his former boss had received.

It seems that everyone, including Mr. R., was aware of the discrepancy. But when his co-workers suggested he demand a higher wage, Mr. R. recoiled visibly. "Money is a way people have of measuring each other," he said, "and I refuse to be measured."

Ms. S. makes her living as an agent, and represents a number of well-known actors. In both the New York theater world and in Hollywood, she has a reputation for being shrewd and tough. Her savvy and stubbornness have frequently enabled her to execute deals for her clients that make them the envy of the industry. Rising stars consider it a coup to get representation by Ms. S.

Earning 10 percent of her clients' income should have made Ms. S. a rich woman. Yet, in her mid-fifties she does not have a great deal of money. A few years back she was swindled into putting most of her savings into an ill-advised business venture, a penny stock scam involving a supposed new miracle drug, which she later admitted "smelled a little fishy from the start."

Ms. T. is a painter who for years turned out new watercolors at a prolific rate. Since her art earned her no money, she made a living working nights as a waitress. A few years ago, however, she got a gallery show and then another. Her work began to catch on, and the next thing she knew she was widely acknowledged as a hot new artist. Soon Ms. T. could afford to quit her waiting job and paint full time. In fact, she could afford to buy a spacious loft, or do just about anything she wanted to do. Ms. T. gave up waiting tables and purchased the loft of her dreams. But she found she could not paint there. She took trips to places she'd always longed to capture on canvas. But when she got to those places, she found she could not paint there either. Ms. T. began to wonder if she should have kept her night job after all.

Mr. V. worked as the pastry chef in a chic restaurant that continually earned excellent reviews from food critics, with particular raves for its desserts. Encouraged by customers and critics alike, Mr. V. ultimately left the restaurant to open his own cafe, funding his entrepreneurial enterprise largely with borrowed money. Upon the cafe's opening, it, too, was touted in the press. But the cafe did not succeed. Mr. V., it turns out, had picked a location where there was no foot traffic and little available parking. Soon he was forced to close up shop; but he decided to give his business another try, and borrowed yet more money. His new neighborhood, however, was practically deserted in the evenings and on weekends. Once again he had to close his doors—this time for good.

Why did these talented, hardworking people end up in such terrible financial distress? Not by mere chance. Each of them was racked by emotional conflicts that resonated in the financial realm.

Mr. R., the magazine editor who refused to be "measured" by monetary standards, revealed a story of growing up in a family and hometown in which no one rewarded him, emotionally or financially, for being himself or doing what he liked to do. The last of three sons born in his family, Mr. R. perceived himself as "the runt of the litter." His older brothers were, in fact, more physically imposing than he—taller, broader, more muscular. Both excelled in a wide range of sports and outdoor activities, and both were praised extensively by a mother and father who seemed to value athletic prowess over intellectual achievement.

Mr. R., small in stature and more intrigued with science and books than with sports, never seemed to garner the accolades his siblings did. Nor did he merit the same level of financial attention from his mother and father. His brothers were more or less continually showered with gifts of athletic equipment and camping gear. Much money was spent on family trips to watch one or the other of them play out-of-town games for their high school teams. Very little was spent in helping Mr. R. pursue his interests.

Later, both Mr. R.'s brothers received athletic scholarships from the local university. Though Mr. R. was a straight-A student, he was not similarly honored. His parents had to help him with funding for college, and it seemed to him they did so only grudgingly.

The result of all this, as Mr. R. put it, was that he decided it was his fate to "accept a supporting role in life rather than a lead." Other people, he felt, were destined to have "all the glory." This, of course, is the attitude he carried with him into the corporate arena. Even when he was elevated at his job from understudy to star, he remained loyal to his scenario by agreeing to an amount of money that was inadequate and unfair.

In Mr. R.'s case, family dynamics (Layer Two of the Money Complex) and the social message (Layer Three) conveyed by the university that gave his brothers, but not him, a free ride, combined to shape a self-defeating financial stance. In his psyche, money was emotionally associated with approval. Since he never got enough of the latter in youth, from his parents or his community, he arranged not to get enough of the latter in adulthood.

. . . .

For Ms. S., money had another key association. She equated it with masculinity. According to this successful agent, her reputation as a hard-nosed dealmaker never sat quite right with her. Though she enjoyed her work immensely, she felt at the same time that it wasn't really seemly for a woman to be so tough and competent when it came to money matters. To her mind, a woman who evidenced savvy about money was not perceived as feminine.

Where did this idea come from? As it turned out, the marriage of Ms. S.'s parents had broken up when her mother's own financial status changed radically. The mother had married and had children at an early age, and for many years being a homemaker was her sole vocation. When Ms. S. was a teenager, however, her mother got a real estate license and promptly "made a bundle." Her husband justified his leaving her for another woman with the explanation that she "didn't need him anymore."

After that, Ms. S. was convinced that men would shy away from women who had the nerve to be financially successful. This attitude caused her much emotional difficulty, as she was always ambivalent about whether or not she wanted to be in a romantic relationship. Obviously, it caused her fiscal difficulty as well.

When Ms. S. lost so much money in a bad investment, her friends and colleagues were astounded. They wondered how anyone so sharp and sophisticated when it came to other people's deals could get swept up in such a bad one herself. Why, they asked, didn't she pore over her own documents as carefully as she would have on a client's behalf? Why didn't her normally foolproof instincts alert her to the fact that she was capitulating to lemminglike enthusiasm, not making a well-considered decision based on facts?

Today, Ms. S. admits that though she allowed herself to earn money for others, she may have felt unentitled to keep her share. Perhaps, she says, she even sabotaged herself in order to be in a position to be rescued by a suitor. "Maybe I thought a damsel in distress would be more likely to find true love than a powerhouse."

In this case, we see how a family "moneygram" (Second Layer) predisposed someone to appropriate a higher layer of the Money Complex (in this case, the Fifth Layer, the Pack-Think Layer) for the acting out of money neurosis.

. . . .

Ms. T., the painter, offered another explanation for her behavior. To her, the pursuit of artistic excellence was something to be kept "totally pure." Like many successful creative people, she was enamored of the process of creation, by the challenge it presented, and by the transcendent state it induced in her. But when recognition and pecuniary reward first came her way, she found she could not sustain a pleasurable state of creation. She was too overcome with guilt.

"I felt that money was going to taint my work," she explained. "And I thought it was wrong, immoral, and utterly bizarre that I should be paid for doing something I loved so much—in fact, for doing something I felt I couldn't have lived without. It was obscene somehow—I mean would you pay somebody to breathe?"

Ms. T.'s use of the words "wrong," "immoral," and "obscene"—words so often used in our culture in association with the attainment of outside-money—here evidenced a deep conflict about inside-money. Whatever came out of her, Ms. T. thought, should be untainted and pure. Money was impure. By receiving money for art, she was, in a sense, soiling herself. Her unwillingness to accept payment for her artwork was a manifestation of a First Layer intrapsychic metaphor—that of "dirty money"—running amok.

. . . .

Mr. V., the pastry chef–cum–entrepreneur, found that, like Mr. R., his conflict was rooted primarily in family history. Mr. V.'s immigrant father was, like his son, a baker. He eked out a living by running a small bakeshop and worked seven days a week to make ends meet. He never stopped explaining to his children how hard it was to make a living. What's more, he never stopped expounding his belief that the greatest disgrace possible was to use credit of any kind for any reason.

When Mr. V. gained repute as a pastry chef in a glamorous restaurant, his father was clearly less than elated. He had envisioned that Mr. V. would take over the family bakeshop. Now he feared he never would. His child had joined, in his eyes, the ranks of those who did not understand that work should mean solely sweat and sacrifice. What an outrage! Here his son did not have to work as hard as father, or put in as many hours, and yet people made a fuss over him. Imagine!

Mr. V.'s announcement to his father that he was opening his own business was greeted with the retort "Now you'll learn how hard it really is. We'll see what happens when you try to go it alone." When the father discovered his son was taking out loans to start up his enterprise, he lost his temper. "Now you're really going to be ruined," he predicted.

Despite his dislike of his father's pessimism, rigidity, and envy, Mr. V. feels very bound to him. Yet today he acknowledges that many of his poor business decisions were made as a result of a self-defeating attempt at filial loyalty.

"Once I took out those loans," he said, "I felt I had to make the money back right away to prove my father wrong. I was so obsessed with making interest payments that I could think of nothing else. I couldn't get a grasp on the numbers. I just knew I wanted to eradicate the debt. So I acted hastily, and, in the end, of course, proved my father right. I couldn't make a go of it. I wonder now if I was really trying to protect my father from the shame of being proven wrong or surpassed by his son."

In this case, we again see how layers of the Money Complex interact. In order to prove the validity of certain family money messages (the Second Layer), Mr. V. developed a hysterical, irrational, and thus ineffective, attitude toward the techniques of money and credit (the Fourth Layer).

. . . .

The specifics of these stories differ. As the histories of these men and women show, various layers of the Money Complex proved particularly powerful in contributing to their prevalent symptom: that of money aversion. But the common theme running through all their money attitudes is the attitude that says, "I do not deserve it."

I do not deserve to have as an adult what I could not have as a child. I do not deserve as a woman to have what rightfully belongs only to men. I do not deserve to be paid for doing something that comes naturally to me. I do not deserve to progress beyond my parents.

In the paradoxical world of money and mind, it can be difficult to state truths categorically, but with very few exceptions, the following is true: Those who believe they do not deserve a fair financial return for their labors will not get one.

When it comes to work, a chimplike adherence to the money motive with disregard for all of work's other potential benefits is dehumanizing. But it is dehumanizing as well to belittle our own needs and disregard practical considerations. It is madness to do everything for money, but it is equally mad to do everything for nothing, or next to nothing.

Doing work one enjoys and being paid sufficiently well for it is the happiest of happy mediums. If you do something for me or sell something to me, and I pay you enough so that you feel gratified and I do not feel cheated, both of us are enhanced. No one loses, and everyone gains.

Would that exchanges of money were always so simple in one's personal life. But, alas, issues of love and money can present even more opportunities for problems than issues of work and money. And that is the subject of the next chapter.

8

. . . .

Money in
the Middle

•

THE MONEY COMPLEX
IN LOVE

. . . .

For money has the power above
The stars and fate to manage love.
—SAMUEL BUTLER

SOME YEARS AGO I had occasion to reside for a week at an
elegant hotel in Siena, Italy. During the course of that week, I
made the acquaintance of Angelo, the hotel's concierge, an
endearingly gracious and meticulous man who took great—and
justifiable—pride in his unflagging ability to make his guests
comfortable and keep his establishment running smoothly.

In addition to his occupation, it turned out that Angelo
had an avocation. One night he divulged to me and to some
guests from New Zealand with whom I had come to strike up
a traveler's intimate but ephemeral bond that he devoted what
spare time he had to the hand-carving of wooden furniture.
Currently, he said, he was working on a set of twelve cabinets,
which he planned, upon their completion, to donate to the
Vatican Museum.

After we'd expressed what must have been sufficient interest, Angelo produced for our inspection photographs of the
cabinets he'd finished so far. Perhaps we were not expecting all
that much—for Angelo had modestly insisted that he was a
novice and told us it was "only from books" that he'd learned

to carve. But we were, in fact, overwhelmed by what we saw. Angelo was evidently blessed with immeasurable natural talent. His wooden cabinets, crafted with painstaking care, were nothing short of breathtaking.

My companions, the New Zealanders, who, I should mention, were still aflush with the glow of a bull market "down under" and whose luggage was already abulge with Venetian glassware and cashmere sweaters from the boutiques of Milan, traded glances, and I knew what would happen next. They offered to purchase some of Angelo's pieces for a lavish sum. Angelo declined with some embarrassment and, I thought, a mild hint of umbrage. The pieces were destined as offerings to the Pope, he said, and that was that.

I cannot say I came to know Angelo all that well, but he did not seem to me to be a self-destructive man. He found his job at the hotel engaging and challenging and was, at least judging from the clothes he wore, the car he drove, and the photographs of his home that he shared with us, more than tolerably well paid for it. There was little doubt, however, that he could have availed himself of far greater sums of money had he been willing to sell his exquisite creations for the high price they would surely command in the marketplace.

Nevertheless, "give" messages resonated strongly in this man's psyche. And in return for proffering his creations, i.e., his money equivalents, to the church, he gained self-affirming feelings more pleasing to him than riches would ever be. All things considered, he did not appear spiritually, artistically, or economically deprived. But he did have a problem.

As Angelo confided to us before our stay ended, his wife was sorely displeased with his decision not to sell any of his cabinets. She did not want him to focus on giving—unless it was to her. How could he be completely happy with the choices he'd made when the woman he loved insisted those choices resulted in her deprivation, and when she relentlessly nagged him to change his ways?

. . . .

Healthy adults, as Freud pointed out, concern themselves largely with the achievement of success in the areas of love and work. Money is a crucial factor in both arenas. But the choices we make about work and money, and indeed any choices we make about money at all, become more complicated when we realize that they affect those we love and those who love us.

People are fond of saying it is a mistake to confuse money with love. Of course, it is a mistake, just as it is a mistake to perceive money strictly in terms of any emotional commodity. Nevertheless, it is naive to think we can completely separate matters of the heart from matters of the purse. The way we feel about and respond to money influences the way we feel about and respond to those with whom we are closest. And of all human relations, marriage is perhaps the one where this truth holds most true.

MARRYING MONEY

When two people marry, they form, among other things, a financial unit, a kind of corporation. That is a social and legal fact, and it is also a psychological one.

Money and marriage have always gone hand in hand. Throughout much of human history, money figured heavily in the pairings of husbands and wives. For centuries, it was quite unthinkable that men and women from different socioeconomic backgrounds should wed. Moreover, it was considered routine in many cultures for parents of prospective brides and grooms to busily concern themselves with matters such as the man's financial prospects and the woman's dowry.

Today, money matters are no less significant to the marital union than they were in the past. Though we like to profess our admiration and approval for love matches, and though we believe, at least in theory, that anyone may marry whomever they choose, regardless of their tax bracket or credit rating, our lofty ideals are not enough to keep money matters from playing a role in romance.

Even at the initial dating phase of a relationship, certain money issues are liable to arise. A spending protocol must be set. Who pays for dinners and movies? Who pays for popcorn at the movies? Both parties will have feelings about whatever accommodations are reached. Are they fair or unfair? Are they too rigid? Were they made with immediate circumstances in mind (like which member of the couple earns what) or influenced by tradition (which may dictate that the man pays for dates regardless)? The feelings will doubtless affect the relationship's course.

As the people involved begin to consider each other as potential lifetime partners, each member of the couple will likely begin to speculate silently about just how much money the other may have. And each begins to form opinions about the way the other deals with money. Why doesn't he tip properly? Is he a penny-pincher? Just how much does she spend on all those clothes? Can't she control herself?

Alas, speculation and opinion are for a long while all one may have to go on. Parents no longer take on the job of garnering financial information on their marriageable children's behalf. And outrightly volunteering or requesting information regarding one another's assets and liabilities is a practice shunned by many a pair of smitten lovers.

For reasons of which we are already aware, money is all too frequently considered an unsuitable topic for detailed discussion. It's crass, it's embarrassing, and so forth. During courtship, additional factors may inhibit conversation about it. Discussions of money certainly have the potential to induce anxiety, and there is nothing like anxiety to quell the fires of passion. Moreover, in our culture, personal money matters are considered deeply private—more private, indeed, than one's sexual history. In delaying the sharing of information on the subject, we can preserve a sense of autonomy, even as we move inexorably toward union.

What's more, in money matters, as in all other matters, people involved in courtship are generally on their best behavior. If they are aware that their particular money attitudes may not be perceived as a plus by the object of their affections, they may attempt to cover them up, or at least tone them down.

Of course, as the wedding day approaches, practical matters generally necessitate the divulging of at least some specifics. Questions of who will pay for what features of the wedding itself, where the couple can afford to live after marriage, and so on will engender a certain amount of nuts-and-bolts money talk and with it a certain amount of stress and perhaps even shock. Suddenly, spouses-to-be may discover that assumptions they made early on were unfounded, that hopes they harbored were unjustified, or that problems they willfully ignored have turned out to be larger than they feared. But, after all, they will likely remind themselves, they are marrying for love, not money. Things will work out.

Things may work out, to be sure, but usually not without some struggle. Once the knot is tied, husbands and wives invariably find that money looms large as a marital issue because each one brings to the marriage perceptions of money that have been many years in the making and that are highly unlikely to change without sincere and dedicated effort.

At any layer of the Money Complex where partners' money-related emotions differ, opportunities for conflict abound. Conflict can center around spouses' prevalent First Layer money metaphors. It is not hard to imagine the type of arguments that might predominate in a household where someone who relates to money as food, and is frantically occupied with getting and spending it, has a mate who relates to money as a precious body product which he cannot bear the thought of giving up. Nor is it difficult to envision the bitter quarrels that might ensue when someone who relates to money as a soothing security blanket and takes comfort in anticipating its regular reappearance (in the form of a weekly paycheck, quarterly dividend statement, or what have you) teams up with a money avoider who somehow always manages to keep money—filth that is!—from coming his way.

Conflict can, and very often does, center around differing Second Layer "moneygram" messages that were transmitted in each spouse's family of origin. A wife from a family with a buy-now-pay-later philosophy is likely to clash with a husband whose parents stressed thrift. A husband from a family which routinely lived well above its means, subscribing to a myth that someday its ship would inevitably come in, is just as likely to clash with a wife whose parents, whatever their actual financial situation, verbally or nonverbally conveyed to their daughter a fear that ruination and abject poverty lurked around every bend. Someone raised in a home where money and gifts were distributed more or less evenhandedly among siblings is likely to have a different feeling about money from one who felt as if he or she was the "underprivileged" child in the family unit.

Naturally, the actual economic standings of each spouse's family of origin can contribute to monetary friction in marriage. A spouse from a wealthy background may well harbor a radically different attitude toward money from a mate reared in the relative poverty of a working-class milieu where different Third Layer social messages were absorbed. Yet there are, of course, many additional Third Layer obstacles other than interclass marriages, such as when spouses respond differently to the "spend" and "give" messages to which they are exposed. Will a couple buy a new car because the neighbors have one—and because the ads for that car are so enticing? Will they attend a local charity ball because it is the "chic" event in town?

Reactions to the techniques and technology of money, which comprise the Fourth Layer of the Money Complex, also provide fertile ground for strife between partners. There is no end to the annoyance that a credit card junkie may feel when faced with a diehard cash-only spender, or that a meticulous record keeper may feel when faced with the plaintive cries of a spouse who insists, "I don't know where the tax receipts are. I don't even know *what* tax receipts are."

Even partners' varying tendencies for being swept up in pack-think, the Fifth Layer of the Money Complex, can lead to trouble. A spouse who cannot quell his enthusiasm for glam-

190

orous schemes and scams may well infuriate a "contrarian" partner with a slow and steady approach to investing. Where will the retirement money be stashed? In earthworm futures or in government bonds?

In chapter 1, an example was given of an internal money dialogue in which a Mr. C. had to decide whether or not to purchase a new computer system. In that dialogue, we saw how different "voices" emanating from the Five Layers of the Money Complex interacted to produce certain behaviors. Now, let's look at an internal dialogue à deux.

SITUATION Mr. and Mrs. Green are giving their only daughter a wedding and must decide how much to budget.

Here are Mrs. Green's thoughts on the situation:

LAYER I (INTRAPSYCHIC) RESPONSE I love to spend money on lavish things. I also love to lavish money on the people I care about. It's so satisfying. After all, what better way is there to show them I *do* care?

LAYER 2 (FAMILY-TRAINING-BASED) RESPONSE My parents scrimped and saved when it came to my wedding. It was an embarrassment I felt I never lived down. I'll show them how it *should* have been done.

LAYER 3 (SOCIAL-TRAINING-BASED) RESPONSE All my daughter's friends who have gotten married this year have had their ceremonies at the country club and used that fabulous new, very expensive caterer. I don't really like his food very much, but I suppose if we don't hire him, people will say we couldn't afford to.

LAYER 4 (TECHNOLOGY-BASED) RESPONSE I know! We can use the cash in my checking account to pay the caterer and then put the wedding dress, the flowers, and as much else as we can on credit cards and worry about it later. This way I won't feel like we're spending so much.

LAYER 5 (PACK-THINK) RESPONSE Besides, the stock market has been going up lately. I heard some financial expert on the radio say we're definitely headed for an all-time high. I wonder who that was? Oh, well, doesn't matter. But good times are surely just around the corner if someone on the radio said so. If we really go overboard for this wedding, we can make some money back investing. At least we could if I could get my husband to give up those boring blue chips and do something exciting.

Obviously, this happy occasion provided Mrs. Green with an excellent opportunity to overextend herself, as is her overwhelming inclination. In her case, each voice of the Money Complex echoed and amplified the others, making for a cacophony of "spend" messages. Predisposed to consumption, and given to equating money with expressions of affection, Mrs. Green had also developed a reaction formation that went against her parents' conservative financial messages. Acutely status-conscious as well, she felt compelled to keep up with her friends and neighbors. When doing so proved beyond her immediate means, she felt comfortable using plastic "funny money," which she did not experience as real, to make up the difference. She even fantasized making a potential killing in the stock market as a means of justifying her expenditures.

One might assume that the outcome of Mrs. Green's deliberations was a foregone conclusion and that her daughter's nuptials were second in splendor only to those of the Prince and Princess of Wales. Indeed that is surely the way things would have gone—were it not for *Mr.* Green's internal dialogue, which went like this:

LAYER I (INTRAPSYCHIC) RESPONSE I would like to give my daughter a nice wedding, but I am always afraid of going overboard. Unless I have a certain amount in my bank account, I find I cannot sleep at night.

LAYER 2 (FAMILY-TRAINING-BASED) RESPONSE Waste not, want not, as Mom and Dad always said.

LAYER 3 (SOCIAL-TRAINING-BASED) RESPONSE It's true all our friends seem to be using that new caterer. I can't stand the niggardly little portions he doles out, and I hate his pretentious soufflés. Still, I suppose my wife is right about this part at least. We hardly want to come off looking like cheapskates in front of the whole community.

LAYER 4 (TECHNOLOGY-BASED) RESPONSE Well, if we have to spend all that money on the caterer, we'll just have to cut back elsewhere. I'm certainly not going to run up any debt. If I even *see* an outstanding balance I can't cover on my credit card bill I get insomnia for two weeks. I know! We'll hire the caterer but have the wedding in the backyard. And my wife can sew a dress for my daughter.

LAYER 5 (PACK-THINK) RESPONSE Yes, we'd really better be careful. Times may get tough. The market's been going up, but that's just wild speculation. I'm glad I've got my blue chips to hang on to, but even they'll devaluate for a while.

In the end, the Greens argued for months about how to proceed. Neither could agree on anything except the fact that the caterer neither of them liked was an absolute necessity. Ultimately, their daughter was married in a backyard ceremony, as opposed to the country club. The dessert served, however, was "pretentious" soufflés, and the bride was garbed in a store-bought wedding dress bought on a credit card—the monthly statement for which caused Mr. Green to pace his hallway in a nocturnal frenzy for weeks on end. No one was entirely pleased, except for the parents of the groom, who had been prepared to foot half the bill and were astonished when no one requested their financial participation. So terrified were Mr. and Mrs. Green of broaching the subject of their assets and liabilities with their new in-laws—both because they deemed such discussion crass and unseemly and because, equating money with self-worth, they were loath to be "judged" by their fiscal bottom line—that they never availed themselves of the solution that readily awaited them.

In marriage, as in one's family of origin, problems may arise not only because of differing points of view about money but also because spouses fail to communicate effectively about it. And, as in one's family of origin, marital partners, knowingly or unknowingly, sometimes use money as a vehicle for making negative emotional communications to each other. Money in marriage can be used to express resentment, competitiveness, and mistrust, and to convey a host of other messages as well.

It can be used to express doubts about the long-term future of the marriage.

"My wife seems to think it's really odd that I won't agree to put any money into joint accounts," says George, married for three years. "It's not that I don't think she is responsible. She is. It's just that I'm a realist. I mean, half of all couples get divorced, right? I'm not saying it will happen, but . . . I've seen my friends go broke. It would be easier this way, cleaner, you know, to split things up with no confusion."

George also insists on filing his taxes separately, though he would likely save money by filing jointly. "Just in case we do get divorced," he says, "who wants to face the prospect of being audited together afterwards?"

It can be used in service of overdependency.

"Sure, I used to handle my own money before I married Bob," says Susan, married for five years, "but I always looked forward to the day I wouldn't have to anymore. Right after the wedding, I said to Bob, 'Here's everything—checkbooks, credit cards, bankbooks. Do what you have to do. I don't want to know.' I don't even let him tell me what he's doing

with our investments. Last time the stock market
took a dive he was obviously a little upset. But I
didn't want to hear about it. It's not that I don't understand about stocks and bonds. I'm pretty smart,
all right. It's just that this is now his domain. Sometimes my husband tries to explain something or
other about our portfolio to me, in case something
should ever happen to him. But I just tell him that
if something should ever happen to him, or if he
should ever leave me or anything, well, that would
be it. I'd just end up in the poorhouse. A charity
case."

*Money can be used to express unwillingness to give the mar-
riage priority over other relationships.*

"My wife and I have been married for thirty-five
years," says Martin, "and throughout all that time
she handled her widowed father's financial affairs.
She would never utter one word to me, though,
about any of those matters. It was always a deep,
dark secret, and if I made even a casual remark
about it, she would accuse me of prying. Recently
my father-in-law died, and my wife went to the
reading of his will without me. She hasn't told me
how much money he left her and she says she's not
planning to. She says that's *still* between her and
her father."

*And all too often it can be offered as a poor substitute for
emotional commitment and physical affection.*

"The year that I spent the most money on gifts
for my ex-wife was the year I was falling in love
with someone else," says Richard, now married for a
second time. "Even before I started having an affair,
I mean when I was just fantasizing about it, I began

buying my wife expensive jewelry for no special occasion. She used to joke that it made her suspicious,
and of course that made me nervous. But instead of
stopping, I felt compelled to buy her more things. I
remember it was in the late autumn that the affair
actually began, and when Christmas came, you
would have thought I'd won the lottery or something. I practically bought out the stores trying to
please her, because I knew I'd end up depriving her
of what she really wanted."

In a marriage, money can be employed to exert control ("If
you love me, you'll let me manage the money") and to create
bondage ("Everything you have is because of me! You'd never
be able to make it on your own"). It can be used as an excuse
to overstep boundaries ("I just happened to open your credit
card bill that came in the mail and I'm wondering how come
you spent forty-two dollars on makeup. You look better without makeup") and as an excuse for avoiding closeness ("I can't
spend more time with you. I'm too busy making money for
us").

Of course, money or its equivalents can also be offered to
a spouse as a kind of reward. Money may be proffered to com-
memorate a goal achieved or to acknowledge a mate who has
been especially helpful or supportive in some fashion. And
certainly money or material gifts may be given as a relatively
straightforward expression of one's abiding overall affection.

Naturally enough, couples who have the least friction
when it comes to money are the ones where both partners'
money-related attitudes, no matter how odd they may be, dove-
tail. A Mr. and Mrs. Hoarder, no matter how the rest of their
acquaintances may view them, will tend to view one another
as "sensible" and "conservative." A Mr. and Mrs. Overspender,
no matter how much anxiety they may cause their creditors,
will likely agree that the Hoarders are a couple of "tightwads"
and that their own freewheeling fiscal philosophy is far more
"normal."

Likewise, couples who agree on an emotional meaning of money can get on smoothly, regardless of how others judge their behavior. If a husband and wife agree that money should be used to express their bondedness with one another and never buy so much as a box of paper clips without an elaborate joint consultation, they may drive everyone they know to distraction, but exist just as merrily as two quirky peas in an off-beat pod.

Yet such merry matches are somewhat rare.

Because of our propensity for self-contradiction where money is at stake, even those couples who enjoy peaceful financial coexistence much of the time may find themselves at serious odds with one another over a matter at once trivial and enormously potent. Should Mr. Hoarder decide, just this once, to splurge on a set of top-of-the-line golf clubs, Mrs. Hoarder may find herself feeling outraged and betrayed. Should Mrs. Overspender, in an atypical fit of economizing, suggest to Mr. Overspender that perhaps their old car will do for another year, he may feel criticized and controlled. Compromise may be the obvious solution, but not everyone finds himself willing or able to hammer out a compromise with a spouse he perceives as suddenly having gone money mad.

Whether money rifts are frequent or infrequent, they usually pack an incendiary wallop. For behind a mask of money troubles there are likely to lurk more deep-seated marital troubles. An unwillingness to hear and respect one another. A fear of openness. A reluctance to state clearly what one wants and expects from a mate—and what one is willing to offer.

As "George" pointed out, in his attempt to justify his preference for total financial autonomy within his own marriage, half of all marriages do indeed end in divorce. Certainly money problems and the Pandora's box of emotional issues to which they are so often tied rank high among the difficulties that can lead couples to consider a permanent parting of the ways. But whether money has been the focal point of problems in the marriage or not, it will almost surely assume a central role once its dissolution is imminent.

For just as money can be employed in relationships as a reward, it can also be used as a powerful instrument of punishment.

MONEY AND THE TALION

The Bible refers to an eye for an eye as fit punishment for an evil deed. Whatever an offender does, he will have done to him in kind. This brand of primitive justice has come to be known as the talion principle. In psychological terms, the talion principle refers to the belief that a wrong deed must be punished (and can thus, in a sense, be "undone") by inflicting an identical wrong on the original wrongdoer.

Talion has to do with retaliation, a subject that is uppermost in many people's minds as they experience the bitter feelings that often accompany a marriage's demise. Dismayed and disillusioned, in the grip of rage or guilt or shame or sorrow, feeling frightened or betrayed, people in the midst of divorce often desire to inflict a penalty upon the person who, to their mind, is responsible for putting them in such a state.

If embittered husbands and wives took the talion principle literally, they might seek to inflict an intangible wound as their due: a broken heart for a broken heart, or a broken spirit in return for the same. But more often than not, the talion principle undergoes something of a transformation. In an attempt to "undo" the wrongs done to them, and to inflict a suitable punishment, spouses' feelings get tagged with dollar amounts. And when soon-to-be-ex-spouses are informed they must "pay" for the withdrawal of their affections, such a communication is generally understood to mean "in cold cash."

But how much, exactly, are dashed hopes worth? What is the correct price for the breaking of a vow? Such questions might confound Solomon, but courts of law must confront them on a routine basis.

It is certainly no news that ours has become an increasingly litigious society. Judges and juries must decide every day how much to "award" for broken legs, smashed fenders, bungled plastic surgery, and inept aluminum siding jobs. We may complain vociferously about the arbitrariness of such decisions, but are there practical alternatives? In a civilized world, we can't simply damage the appendages or the automobile of someone who damaged ours, nor is it likely we would be afforded the opportunity to perform retaliatory plastic surgery or aluminum siding jobs ourselves, no matter how angry or disappointed we are.

Yet, increasingly, judges and juries are also being asked to make decisions that in effect require the affixing of a price tag to an intangible emotion. And divorce is certainly not the only situation where emotionally connected individuals with an ax to grind have come to invoke a financial talion.

Children have sued their parents for "wrongful upbringing." ("Give me money because you failed to help me thrive.") A high school girl has sued an erstwhile boyfriend for standing her up for the senior prom. ("Give me money because I'm *mortified.*") A mistress has sued her lover's wife for "alienation of affection." ("Give me money because, well ... *because.*")

In the mid-1980s, in a particularly diverting lawsuit, Joan and Robert Postel, the River House neighbors of media-dubbed "Wall Street king" John Gutfreund (which is, somewhat ironically, translated as "good friend") and his wife, Susan, filed for injunctive relief and sought monetary damages totaling $35.5 million in response to the proposed hoisting of a Christmas tree into the Gutfreund apartment via the penthouse roof terrace. "Perhaps if the [Postels] had been invited to the royal Christmas dinner," writer David Michaelis mused in his *Manhattan, inc.* article on the incident, "the trouble never would have started." Perhaps, then, this was really a case where the message was "Give me *lots of* money because you snubbed me."

According to Michaelis, the two families involved in the now infamous Nutcracker Suit, "never spoke directly to one another about the Christmas tree." One wonders how much trouble could have been avoided had they simply made use of a tried and true, free-of-charge technique—the spirited neighborly shouting match—to vent their mutual frustration. Indeed one wonders how many lawsuits could be nipped in the bud if people were willing to communicate their complaints and disappointments to one another in plain words instead of hiring attorneys to do so in legalese.

Yet more and more, it seems to have become socially permissible to say, "Give me money, because you are responsible for my having feelings I don't want to have." Where money-as-talion attitudes will ultimately lead no one knows. Only one thing is certain, and that is that they are not likely to disappear.

The connection between revenge, reward, money, and the law is very old indeed. Consider: There is one legal instrument we have long employed to convey emotional messages in financial terms. That is the last will and testament.

WILLING IT

Throughout our lives, at each developmental stage from childhood to old age, money gets in the middle of virtually every close personal relationship we have. While we are alive, we have the option of conveying affection and approval by bestowing money or its equivalents not just upon spouses but upon parents, siblings, children, friends, and strange as it may seem, even pets.

While we live, we naturally also have the option of conveying anger and disapproval by denying our loved ones both money itself and the niceties money can buy.

A father may say to a son, "No new baseball glove for you, Billy, you've been a bad boy."

A husband may say to a wife, "Jessica, you've been flirting with the butler again. A new Rolls is out of the question."

A master may say to his cocker spaniel, "Spunky, you chewed up my shoes! Forget that new futon, it's back to sleeping on the floor."

But, of course, life is complicated, and relationships are subject to feedback loops. Little Billy may cry. Jessica may hurl a Wedgwood plate across the parlor. Spunky may sulk—or so his owner might imagine.

We may feel guilty for depriving those we care about. We may fear that their deprivation will result in our loss of their love and admiration. We may waffle and hedge and, ultimately, change our minds. But there comes a time when we have the opportunity to make a final decision about what we will do with our money and with the treasures our money has bought.

It is all too true that there are no luggage racks on hearses. And we all know that, unlike Tutankhamen, we cannot take it with us. But many of us avail ourselves of the opportunity to make one last financial gesture. We allocate our "leftover" money so as to let those who survive us know how we really felt about them.

The messages contained in wills, like other emotional-financial messges, are made on many levels. Some are straightforward, their meaning crystal clear. Such messages are sometimes specifically crafted to hurt, to reiterate or accentuate anger that one has harbored throughout one's lifetime.

A mother of four leaves everything she has to her youngest daughter. Her children have known all along that this last child was her favorite, the only one, their mother always said, "who cares, appreciates, and respects me." The will confirms the mother's prejudice and magnifies the hurt of her neglected offspring.

A father disinherits his son, an only child, bequeathing the bulk of his money and property to a charitable foundation and the remainder of it to a trust designated to care for his cat, Whiskers. If there was ever any doubt that the father's lifelong reproach to his son that he was an irresponsible "good-for-nothing" would resonate throughout his child's lifetime, the will has wiped that doubt away.

We hear and read much about relatives rebuffed from beyond the grave by this or that celebrity or multimillionaire. We remember well the most expensive will contest in U.S. history, wherein Seward Johnson's children sued his third wife, and former maid, Basia, to whom he left virtually his entire $500 million estate. We remember that actress Joan Crawford's will specifically disinherited her children "for reasons which are well known to them" (perhaps prompting her daughter's best-selling retort, *Mommie Dearest*). And we may recall that Conrad Hilton disinherited his children and grandchildren, causing his son Barron to enter into an agonizing ten-year battle with the Catholic nuns whose work his father's megamillions were pledged to support.

Though they generally do not make the tabloids, will contests among the nonwealthy are by no means uncommon. But regardless of how much money is at stake, even if a challenge to a will succeeds, the challenger has not completely erased the talion effect. The money may be his, but the message is still the same: "I didn't *want* you to have it. I didn't feel you deserved it."

Of course, not all final money messages are messages of revenge. Some are not meant to harm but to heal, and they do not invoke the talion. A will can be an instrument of apology and of amends, conveying feelings of love and of support that, for whatever reasons, one was unable to express face-to-face.

A childless woman leaves equal shares of her fortune to all her nieces and nephews, even the children of the sister from whom she has been estranged for twenty years.

A father who has always scoffed at a daughter's ambitions to become a doctor turns out to have allocated $50,000 "for the completion of her medical education."

In addition to straightforward communications, one's last financial-emotional communication may include "unspoken" components. No matter how carefully its clauses are spelled out, a will may also have a way of saying things between the lines.

A will may, for example, convey messages to family members by way of its structure, by way of omissions, or by way of naming a particular executor to enforce the deceased's last wishes. Such "unspoken" messages may have long-term impacts on heirs, and may serve to perpetuate or to radically alter pre-existing family dynamics.

"When I was a child," says Marissa, thirty-five, "I remember hearing my parents speculating in whispers about how much money they might come into when my mother's father, a rather wealthy man, died. The messages my grandfather himself gave us about that subject were mixed. He would always say, 'I'm not going to talk about my money,' and sometimes he would make cryptic remarks like 'Never assume anything.' But at other times he would assure us that we 'would never have a care.' In our heart of hearts, I think we all believed there was a big inheritance destined for us. But when he died, we found that there was not nearly as much as we'd expected. The worst part was that the inordinate number of trusts he set up and the convoluted instructions he gave regarding them made everything so confusing that nearly all the money went to the lawyers who tried to figure things out. Grandfather left fifteen trusts in all, and the bank he named as executor said there wasn't enough left to justify the administration fees. It was a mess. In his death he left us just as confused as we were when he was living. In a way he still was refusing to be clear on the subject of money."

"My Uncle Bob and I were more like father and son than uncle and nephew," says Marc, forty-two. "Even though Bob had a real son, William, it seemed to me that they never really hit it off. Bob was a self-made man who started out as a butcher and ended up owning a chain of grocery stores. When he made it big, he developed a talent for spending big. He would drive around in limousines, smoke expensive cigars, drink champagne, and give lavish parties. I was always by his side, and it was always assumed by everyone, including my own parents, that my future was happily assured. One day, when I was fifteen, in the middle of his own birthday party Uncle Bob had a heart attack and died instantly. All his money, except for $25,000 due me, flat out, when I turned eighteen, was left in trust for his real son. When I turned eighteen, I went through my inheritance fast, spending it as furiously as I imagined Uncle Bob would have. Then I went through years of financial paralysis, convinced that somehow there had been a mistake that would be uncovered and corrected, and that sooner or later I would make my fortune through the dead. Meanwhile, William's trusts thrived, and with the interest earned on his inherited investments, he, too, started a booming business. One day William surprised me by telling me he'd learned all about finance at his father's knee. I was shocked. Uncle Bob had taught me spending talents, but not earning or planning talents. Those he reserved for his flesh and blood. His will preserved that strange split past his dying day."

"I have two sisters," says Janet, fifty-nine, "and we were always very close until my parents died. Now neither I nor my younger sister, Evelyn, are speaking to our eldest sister, Iris. My father made her executor of his will, and that was the end of our friendship. Iris was always ridiculously tight with money. It kills her to spend a cent. Now, maybe that's why my father made her executor, because he felt she would preserve his money—which, I should add, there wasn't terribly much of to begin with— the longest. Maybe this was his way of watching over us and trying to protect us. But Iris has always been so excessively stingy. Didn't he know that she would do everything in her power to keep us from getting our hands on so much as a dime? Dad was always thrifty himself, always disapproving if Evelyn or I treated ourselves to anything above and beyond bare necessities. Is this his way of 'disciplining' us still?"

It is hard to know exactly what the father of Janet, Evelyn, and Iris had in mind when he constructed his last money message to his daughters. Perhaps his primary intent was to protect them; perhaps it was to punish them. Most likely he consciously intended to do one thing and unconsciously intended to do the other. Both conscious and unconscious intentions can be conveyed simultaneously in our final money messages, just as they can be in the ones we communicate all our lives.

. . . .

Henny Youngman used to wisecrack, "I've got all the money I'll ever need if I die by four o'clock." Things might be simple indeed if we could all somehow arrange to depart this world with the last of our bills paid up, the last of our money spent. Evened up with a totally balanced ledger sheet. But things rarely work out that way. Most of us will die with some assets to distribute, and how we ready ourselves—or do not ready ourselves—to part with our money says much about what we have learned, or not learned, about coming to terms with the Money Complex in our lifetime.

If one has always lived with an unshakable belief that the function of money is to allow its possessor to exert power and control over others, one may attempt to influence the future of one's family through ironclad unbreakable trusts. Or one may leave a last will and testament filled with clauses and conditions compelling an heir's obedience ("Forty thousand to my son, Hank, provided he doesn't marry his atrocious girlfriend, Peaches"). If one ages holding on to the notion that the purpose of money is to glorify the self, one may make extravagant, inordinate bequests aimed at assuring posthumous fame. ("I leave nothing to my wife, but four million to the Ivy League school that wouldn't let me in—provided they name a football stadium after me.")

If one has long nursed a disdain for money, a belief that it is indeed worthless filth, he may die intestate—that is, having made no last will and testament at all. In the bargain, of course, he will likely create chaos among his progeny, and make sure everyone ends up losing. So, one is tempted to ask, is the deceased's contempt really for money, or for those he left behind?

But how can we really say? After all, the dynamics of the two relationships are inextricably intertwined. Again, we see how the way we experience money cannot help but have a bearing on how we experience and interact with other people.

One of the common replies to the question "How much money, ideally, would you like to have?" is "Enough to tell everyone else to go stuff it." But no amount of money would make such a stance possible, much less truly desirable. It is true that people need to rely on money. It is also true that people need to rely on other people. Often, people need to rely on one another's money. That, of course, is when things get sticky.

To long for a perfect relationship with money would be unrealistic. As we know, money can, at times, seem frustrating, maddening, and incomprehensible. It would be equally unrealistic to long for a perfect relationship with our fellow humans—also known to be frustrating, maddening, and incomprehensible. But if we can improve our relationship with money, it follows that our other relationships, including the one we have with ourselves, will prosper.

So, just what can we do to unravel our personal Money Complex and foster a healthier relationship with money? And what can we do to help our children have a healthier relationship to it as well? These are the subjects of the next, and final, chapter.

4
PART

- - - - - - - - -

Getting
a Grip
•
Toward
a Reasonable
Relationship
with Money

- - - - - - - - -

9

. . . .

Smart
Money

. . . .

Blessed is the man who has both mind and money, for he
employs the latter well.

—MENANDER

In the land of the blind, the one-eyed man is king.
—TRADER ADDRESSING 1985 CLASS OF
SALOMON BROTHERS TRAINEES

THE OFFICE of Currency Standards, a division of the U.S.
Treasury Department's Bureau of Printing and Engraving, has a
mandate to assist individuals and institutions whose money
has been accidentally damaged in the course of events. Each
day, the OCS reviews hundreds of requests for replacement of
bills that have been soaked in the rinse cycle, mashed by a
trash compactor, or chewed up by the family pet. OCS employees like to tell the story of the farmer whose cow swallowed his
wallet. They also like to warn people to be careful with their
money. The biggest problem with money these days, they contend, is that when it accidentally gets wet, people try to dry it
out in a microwave.

If that were really the biggest problem with money, of
course, the world would be a far simpler place. But the problematical permutations offered by money are nearly limitless.

One could go on more or less indefinitely citing examples
of people caught in the throes of money hunger, money envy,
money hoarding, money worship, money anxiety, money aver-

sion, money martyrdom, money phobia, money magic, and any number of variations on these themes. Even so, someone would likely object that the list did not include their Uncle Mo, who peers into their refrigerator whenever he stops by to inquire how much they paid for the blueberries; or their Aunt Zelda, who has buried a chest of Susan B. Anthony dollars in her backyard in the belief that in the postnuclear age, when women rule the world, they will be the only form of legal tender.

But there comes a point where dwelling on specific examples becomes not only impractical but less than efficacious. Some general guidelines must be sought if the Money Complex is ever to be tackled.

Throughout this book, the phenomenon of the Money Complex has been investigated from the bottom up, i.e., from its deepest and densest layer, the intrapsychic layer, upward through the tiers that develop later in one's life. But if we are going to attempt the deconstruction of our own personal Money Complex—and that is the purpose of this chapter—the best way to do so is not from the bottom up but from the top down. For that will allow us to start with the "simpler" part.

The later in life that eccentricities and neuroses are developed, the closer their source is to the surface of consciousness and the more amenable they are to revision. The earlier in life any sort of pathology takes root, the more intractable it tends to be. Thus, the uppermost layers of the Money Complex will prove most amenable to being reached through recall and reason and most responsive to cognitive, pragmatic strategies. The lowermost, as we shall see, are more readily reached through the clues contained in potently experienced feelings and speculative reconstruction. It is only from the vantage point of an examined adulthood that we can begin to speculate about which family "moneygrams" and primal metaphors shaped our money attitudes.

In the section that follows, strategies for examining and contending with each layer of the Money Complex are offered. You will note they are called strategies, not solutions. For the Money Complex is not a puzzle we can solve once and for all, but rather a perennial quandary we must deal with on an ongoing basis.

Preceding each group of strategies are questions that are designed to help you ascertain whether or not you are particularly susceptible to a given layer of the Money Complex, i.e., whether or not a "weak spot" exists at any of its five layers that may be preventing you from coping with money in a primarily rational and ego-oriented way. As you answer the questions, however, also bear this in mind: The greater one's *in*ability to address any particular aspect of the subject of money calmly and clearly, the greater the likelihood that that aspect comprises an emotional "weak spot." Thus, when attempting to determine where your most acute money weaknesses lie, it is wise to pay attention to the very areas you may be disinclined to think about or discuss—or where you notice that what discussion you *do* engage in takes the form of demands, complaints, and redundant exclamations.

Transforming one's money attitudes is no easy task, and doing so will certainly not prove a cure-all for all of one's problems, financial or otherwise. Obviously, attitude is not the *single* determinant of one's financial destiny. Not all people are afforded the same opportunity to accumulate and employ money wisely—or, for that matter, unwisely. Still, even a moderate degree of success in achieving awareness of one's attitudes and even a modicum of movement toward the reality principle where money is concerned may nevertheless have profound ramifications—not only in the purely fiscal arena but in other arenas as well, particularly in the realms of love and work. Like a pebble tossed in a pond, one's relationship to money has a ripple effect.

TOWARD TRANSFORMING
MONEY ATTITUDES

LAYER 5: PACK-THINK The following questions are meant to help you ascertain if you are particularly susceptible to being caught up in crowd-generated emotion when it comes to making choices about where to invest your money.

SPOTTING A WEAK SPOT

1 Are you more likely to be persuaded to make an investment by anecdotal material than by facts and figures?

2 Are you inclined to go ahead and jump on a good deal even when only sketchy information about its particulars is available?

3 Do you tend to dwell on single dramatic occurrences rather than examine the big picture?

4 Are you generally averse to financial risk-taking unless several other people take the risk along with you?

5 When it comes to investments, do you cheerfully ignore the odds when they are not in your favor?

6 Do you tend to wipe all doubts about an investment out of your mind after you have made the decision to invest?

7 Will you throw good money after bad rather than admit to making a mistake?

8 Have you ever purchased an art object, antique, or other collectible you found truly unappealing, based on someone else's assurance that it would have great resale value?

9 Do you tend to be awestruck by financial forecasters and other self-appointed or media-anointed market pundits?

10 Have you ever been swindled in a financial deal?

11 Do you frequently daydream about monetary windfalls?

12 Are you likely to feel overwhelmingly envious or forlorn if a friend makes a profit from an investment you missed out on?

13 Would you describe yourself as impatient by nature?

14 Are you easily excitable and/or easily discouraged?

15 Would you describe yourself as easily goaded by others into doing things your instincts warn you against?

16 Do you feel secure in your point of view only when many others seem to share it and validate it?

17 Do you tend to blame others for your mistakes?

18 Are you reluctant to follow your hunches if other people tell you they're "crazy"?

19 Would you describe yourself as extremely superstitious?

20 Do you sometimes secretly wish someone would make all life's important decisions for you?

STRATEGIES

Naturally, most people will answer yes to some of the foregoing questions. The world is filled with a great many more followers than leaders. And it can often be exceedingly unnerving to stick with an unpopular viewpoint in the face of mass derision. Most of us tend to be at least a tiny bit impatient and superstitious, at least under certain circumstances. But if you have responded in the affirmative to more than half of these questions, chances are you are particularly susceptible to being swept along with the tide of popular opinion, even when that tide carries you toward your own fiscal demise.

Here are some tactics to help you temper this tendency:

• Cultivate a healthy skepticism. Remember that most anecdotes one hears about another's investments contain an element of the investor's personal mythology. Remember, too, that statistics can often be made to indicate whatever their compiler wishes them to indicate. And *remember most of all* not to underestimate the role of random events and the "chaos factor" inherent in all systems, financial and otherwise.

- Try to slow down your knee-jerk reactions to financial events and world events in general. When a market crash or surge occurs, when the yen or the mark takes a nosedive, or when a "breakthrough" discovery is touted, ask yourself, "What is really happening? What does it mean to me? What can I do about it? What am I willing to risk in order to do something about it? What are the consequences likely to be?"

- Remain open to feedback and to new information after you have committed your money to a stock or scheme of any sort. If the information does not bode well for your investment, make your next decisions accordingly. In the long run, he who notices a sudden leak in a boat and grabs for a life preserver will look less foolish than he who goes down with a sinking ship.

- Consider long-term track records when choosing investment advisers and beware of what mathematician John Allen Paulos terms "the Jeane Dixon effect" (named for the celebrity astrologer), whereby someone's "relatively few predictions are heralded and therefore widely remembered."

- Whenever you feel sorely tempted to dance to a given financial guru's tune, first arrange to expose yourself to the opinion of a guru who is saying exactly the *opposite* of what yours is saying. It should prove easy enough to find one. For every ebullient speculator and wishful thinker, there is also a hysterical doomsayer crying, "The end is near! The markets are going to hell in a handbasket! America is going to hell in a Honda! Take your money out of mutual funds and stick it in a sock!" As *New York Times* economics reporter Peter Passell has written, "A single economic development can be interpreted as a godsend or a disaster, depending on the interpreter's frame of reference."

- Try to remember that people who make long-term economic predictions are just that: *people* making *predictions*, not sorcerers gazing into infallible crystal balls. (You might want to keep in mind the following joke, which economists themselves enjoy telling when they gather together: Albert Einstein dies and goes to heaven, where he asks three angels their I.Q.s. The first says 190. "Wonderful," says Einstein. "We will have long talks on my theory of relativity." The second says 151. "Very respectable," says Einstein. "I shall enjoy talking with you about the prospects for world peace." The third angel says his I.Q. is 82. So Einstein asks him, "What do you think the economy will do next year?"

• Read up on contrarianism and learn a bit about some of the people who have employed this as a successful investment strategy.

• Try to invest in things that have intrinsic value that will stand up over time—even if those things temporarily fall out of favor with the masses.

Now go back and review Questions 11 to 21. This time, think of them as a distinct subgroup. Notice that these questions have to do with some general personality traits. If you answered affirmatively to a majority of them, consider that your predisposition to pack-think in the financial area may be but a small part of the problems you face in your life as a result of your tendency to take precipitous action spurred by fantasy, envy, anxiety, and/or self-doubt.

If you answered yes to Question 11:

• You need to address your fantasy that what you need will appear by magic rather than by effort. Take it to its logical conclusion. Do you want to spend your life waiting for—as they used to say on "Laugh-In"—the "fickle finger of fate"?

If you answered yes to Question 12:

• You need to address why you are more concerned with getting in on what others have than with arranging to get your own realistic needs met in an appropriate way.

If you answered yes to Questions 13 to 15:

• You need to *relax and take your time.* A truly wonderful opportunity of any sort, financial or otherwise, should stand up to scrutiny. Allow yourself the luxury of mulling over your decisions. Do not bend to pressure, self-imposed or imposed by others, to act hastily.

If you answered yes to Questions 16 to 21:

• You need to *get comfortable with your own sense of judgment.* Try to bolster confidence in your personal decision-making powers by recalling times in your life when you were successful at any endeavor due to independence and/or originality. Consider what changes you can make in your life that will make you feel better about yourself overall (this might be anything from losing weight to earning a particular academic degree to expressing a feeling to someone that you never had the nerve to express before). Once you are more sure of yourself you will be less likely to relinquish responsibility for your own life—in its financial and nonfinancial aspects.

LAYER 4: TECHNOLOGY-BASED RESPONSES This section is meant to help you determine whether your reactions to modern money and credit instruments, and to the routine chores incumbent in contemporary money management, are significant factors in shaping any harmful money attitudes you may have—specifically "I don't know" and/or "I don't care" attitudes.

SPOTTING A WEAK SPOT

1 Do you feel exceedingly nervous when facing such financial "rites of passage" as real estate closings, contract signings, pension plan enrollments, and so on?

2 Do you procrastinate when it comes to filling out loan applications, tax forms, and the like to the point where your lateness ends up costing you penalties, endangering deals, and so forth?

3 Do you find yourself obsessed and overwhelmed by what-if worst-case scenarios such as "What if I live too long and my money runs out?" "What if I die too soon and leave my loved ones insolvent?" or "What if an anvil falls on my head and I end up in a coma and can't pay my bills?"

4 Or, conversely, do you find yourself unable to contemplate even the slightest possibility of personal financial catastrophe and insist "That will never happen to me"?

5 Are you obsessed and overwhelmed with fears that humans and computers will make costly (costly to you, that is) errors concerning your money, that your bank will go belly up just in time for the FDIC insurance fund to run out, that your automatically deposited salary will somehow vanish on its electronic route from your employer to your checking account?

6 Or, conversely, do you trust implicitly that your bank will always send you entirely accurate statements, that the IRS will always be correct as to how much money you owe, that your automatically deposited pay will always arrive in your account on the day it's supposed to—in short, that those who handle money for a living and their machines are infallible?

7 Do you throw away receipts of financial transactions, cancelled checks, insurance and pension statements? Or do you ball them up and save them in various closets, drawers, and shopping bags?

8 Do you successfully put thoughts of financial matters out of your head all day but find yourself waking up in the middle of the night plagued with monetary concerns?

9 Do you frequently complain that money matters are boring?

10 Do you secretly believe you would be happier living in a society where money per se did not exist?

11 Are you completely oblivious to the fine print in credit agreements?

12 Do you habitually find yourself charging items on credit cards without any thought as to whether you can realistically pay them off and how long repayment will take?

13 Do you juggle line-of-credit accounts, using one to pay off another?

14 Would you be willing to consolidate your debts to alleviate your paperwork load, even if doing so meant taking on a larger debt?

15 Do you ever enter into financial "blackouts" or "trances" where you splurge on a number of items and don't remember how much you spent?

16 Do you leave mail unopened if you believe it contains bills you can't pay?

17 Do you believe no one will really be hurt if you default on your debts?

18 Do you rationalize overdebting by reminding yourself of all the other people (corporations, countries, etc.) that are in the red?

STRATEGIES

Since we are dealing with two separate attitudes here—albeit separate attitudes that often appear in tandem—let us deal with the questions in this section in terms of two subgroups. Look at Questions 1 to 10. They address reactions to some of the more confusing, overwhelming, and frightening aspects of money as we know it today and are meant to determine whether or not you are prone to an "I don't know" money attitude. Once again, it would be most unusual for anyone to be able to answer negatively to all of these questions. The complexities of routine money management in the contemporary world can indeed be mind-boggling. It is tempting to throw up one's hands and cry, "Uncle." But responding yes to more than half of these questions means you are deliberately avoiding tending to certain critical financial affairs, probably in an attempt to avoid unpleasant feelings. In the short run, you may feel less agitated ignoring money matters. In the long run, however, you will experience much *more* agitation if you do so. Your financial life is out of control. You need to begin to show a willingness to take control.

If you responded yes to a majority of Questions 1 to 10:

• Begin to get a grasp on money matters by tackling one chore at a time. If you don't know how to balance a checkbook, start by learning that. Once you feel comfortable doing so, allow yourself to discover certain financial facts of life as they relate to you. Start slowly. Add up how much you're paying in annual credit card fees. Discover how much your IRA is currently worth (you'll probably find the information in one of those unopened envelopes in the back of your desk drawer or under your bed). Determine the cash value of your life insurance (another unopened envelope).

• Develop some sort of system for keeping financial records and receipts. If you've long resisted this concept, you will not likely cotton to the idea of alphabetizing them in a file cabinet. So do something less drastic. Put them all in a shopping bag if you like, but make certain it's the same shopping bag each time—one that you have easy access to and one that is unlikely to find itself the victim of household mishaps (the basement flood, the curious two-year-old).

• Consider engaging an accountant or money manager to assist you with the bulk of your paperwork. Word of mouth is generally an excellent way to locate suitable candidates. Solicit recommendations from those who have financial situations and requirements similar to your own.

• When interviewing candidates for accountants or money managers, be sure to ask at least one question to which you know the answer (there must be one!).

• Do not engage anyone with whom you do not feel comfortable or do not have a good "gut feeling" about. Shop around until you find someone you believe is capable of understanding how your mind works (yes, your messy, perplexed, and imperfect mind) and of dealing with you in a nonjudgmental fashion. The right "chemistry" is vital.

• But remember, the key word here is *assist*. You are looking for someone to *assist* you with money matters. No one should be given carte blanche to handle your financial affairs. No matter how much you like and trust him, check in with him on a regular basis. Request documentation of any action he takes on your behalf. Participate in the decision-making process.

• Allow yourself to consider the possibility that financial disaster can, in fact, strike. Put what fail-safe mechanisms you can in place, but then relax. Dwelling on the anticipation of calamity does *not* assure that calamity will not befall one. And a great deal of worry is no substitute for a little bit of prudence.

• Swallow with a grain of salt advertisements for investment funds and insurance companies that employ dramatic scare tactics and incite chronic worry. Photographs of a house that looks remarkably like yours floating out to sea or of a baby that strongly resembles your newborn contemplating how Mommy and Daddy will ever afford his college tuition are crafted to increase money anxiety and money guilt. The products such ads are selling may be fine ones. You may want them, even need them. But don't sign up in a fit of induced terror.

• Face this: Sooner or later you are likely to be the victim of a human or computer error that causes a good check to bounce, a bank deposit to go unrecorded, or a surly letter from the IRS to drop on your desk. Recognize that the process of resolving this error will be time-consuming, frustrating, and generally unpleasant. But recognize that you *will* survive.

• Face this, too: For you, money management may always be a somewhat "boring" endeavor. No one will dispute that listening to a symphony, catching a wave, or falling in love is likely to be more fun than comparing interest rates on various CD's. So what? Lots of essential tasks are less than scintillating. Brushing one's teeth, sorting one's trash for recycling, renewing one's driver's license, are not exactly high up on the Thrill and Excitement Scale. That does not mean they should be neglected. The sooner and more efficiently such matters are attended to, the more time there will be for life's deepest pleasures (the ones that really are, for the most part, free).

Now look at Questions 11 to 18. Answering yes to any of these questions may mean you are guilty of an "I don't care" attitude when it comes to spending and debting. Remember, today's credit instruments and techniques tend to aid and abet such an attitude. To offset them:

• Force yourself to read any credit agreement you sign. Ask yourself this question with regard to them all: "If I borrow $1,000 under this agreement and do not pay back any principal for one year, what will it cost me? What about two years?" The answers may shock you into a more realistic approach to debting.

• If the terms of a credit agreement confuse you, insist on clarification. If you are still uncertain, contact the Consumer Credit Counsel.

• Add up what you pay in annual fees for credit cards. Determine which cards you can eliminate.

• Consider leaving your credit cards home when you shop, reserving them only for times when not having them will lead to inordinate inconvenience. Decide ahead of time on a spending ceiling and carry cash up to that amount.

• Consider eliminating credit cards from your life altogether. Yes, this *will* mean letting yourself in for some discouraging run-ins with the system. The best way to cope with resulting inconveniences is by anticipating them and planning ahead as best you can. If you need to rent a car and have no credit cards, call the rental company in advance of your trip. Explain that you choose not to use credit cards, but that you would like to give them your business. Ask for their assistance in making the necessary arrangements. Be sure to get the name and title of the person with whom you speak.

• Avoid Band-Aid solutions to your debting problems. Never consolidate debt if doing so is costly. Open all bills when you receive them.

• Try not to use as role models people (or corporations or countries) that seem to debt and get away with it. That is buying into delusion. Reread Aesop's fable of "The Grasshopper and the Ant." The world is full of grasshoppers, but you need not be one.

• Last but most assuredly not least, remember that overdebting, while assisted by the Fourth Layer of the Money Complex, often begins in the first place because of "weak spots" at deeper levels. Be sure to answer the questions in Layers 3, 2, and 1.

LAYER 3: SOCIAL-TRAINING-BASED RESPONSES These questions are meant to help you ascertain whether your susceptibility to particular social money messages is a factor in shaping irrational money attitudes.

SPOTTING A WEAK SPOT

I Do you find yourself scrutinizing new acquaintances to see what kind of plates they serve dinner on, what color credit card they use in a restaurant, whether or not they wear designer clothes, and whether their jewelry is real or costume?

2 Do you notice yourself feeling superior or inferior to them based on the results of your "survey"?

3 Have you ever found yourself dressing in such a manner as to "fool" people into thinking you are wealthier than you actually are?

4 Do you feel duped when you discover that someone who communicates "I am wealthy" through dress and demeanor turns out to be less well-off than you suspected?

5 Have you ever caught yourself behaving obsequiously toward a person known to have a great deal of money?

6 Do you frequently watch TV shows and read magazine articles that feature profiles of the "rich and famous"?

7 Do most of your friends make as much money or more money than you? Have less financially successful friends tended to fall by the wayside as your income increases?

8 Do you attempt to "keep up with the Joneses" even when you know that doing so will jeopardize your financial security?

9 Does a day rarely go by when you do not find yourself envying others for things they have bought with their money?

10 Do you feel gratified when you know that someone envies you for material advantages you may possess?

11 Do you consider yourself easily influenced by advertising?

12 Do you believe that name-brand products are always superior to generic products?

13 Do you enjoy being in situations where you are the target of sales pitches (e.g., do you tune into Home Shopping Network; do you peruse most of the ads in magazines)?

14 Can you be easily pressured into making a charitable donation you don't really want to make if a neighbor, colleague, or employer of yours solicits you?

15 Have you ever given more than you could really spare to a charitable cause in order to "save face" in your community?

16 Have you ever borrowed money (say, on a line of credit attached to one of your credit cards) in order to make a donation?

STRATEGIES

Unless you were brought up on a desert island or were a feral child raised by wolves, you will most assuredly respond to some of these in the affirmative. Man is a social animal, and money is a social instrument. What's more, money is an entity whose function and very essence depend on relative quantity. We cannot help but think of our money in relation to other people's money. It is only natural to have feelings about whether we have more of it or less of it than those in our proximity—and given the reach of mass media, it can be argued that virtually everyone is "in our proximity" today.

The reach of status-conscious advertising and solicitation is, of course, similarly universal. It's hard to find anyone who hasn't been at one time or another tempted to buy a product because of an economic message with which that product is associated, or tempted to give or overgive to a "good cause" because of the status that action confers. But beyond a certain point, susceptibility to community and media influence, when it comes to making spending or giving decisions, can result in serious harm to one's financial health.

If you answered yes to a majority of Questions 1 to 10:

• Think about what it really is you want when you set out to convey clues that say to those around you, "I am financially successful." As Veblen put it, the "transient good opinion [of one's neighbors and acquaintances] has a high degree of utility." To a certain degree, it can make good business sense to convey economic messages of success to one's clients or business associates, or to anyone whose impression of you as an economic "winner" can help you achieve a higher income, if that's what you're after. Investments in handsome office furniture or a new leather briefcase may sometimes serve as just that: investments. But if you are surrounding yourself with expensive accoutrements, dressing a certain way, or serving dinner on a particular kind of china in the hopes of winning lasting and meaningful friendships—the kind where people stick with each other through thick and thin—you are wasting your money.

• Try to be aware, as they occur, of impulses you may have to fawn over someone you perceive as having a great deal more money than you. Such ingratiating behavior will ultimately make you feel demeaned. Checking these impulses can be difficult, given our complex attitudes toward the rich, and our tendencies to treat them like royalty, but awareness of an attitude is always the first step toward tempering it. It's true that F. Scott Fitzgerald said that the rich are different. But remember what W. C. Fields said: "A rich man is nothing but a poor man with money."

• Try to realize that standing agog in the face of the wealthy in the end demeans them as well as you. As Laura Rockefeller confided in an interview with Vance Packard, "The more I cared about the person I was speaking to, the more I was tempted to look away when I spoke my name because I could not bear to see myself disappear in their eyes."

• Mitigate chronic envy by trying to learn from the people you envy. If they have something you want, see if you can discover how they got it. Make them your role models and not your enemies. Admire them, don't fear them.

• Remind yourself that while money can indeed confer prestige on those who have it, it does not automatically confer dignity. And while it can confer certain kinds of power, it does not automatically confer the power that comes from integrity in the truest sense of the word. To have integrity is to be intact, to feel in possession of oneself, not of *things*.

• Remember that while ascribing value to oneself or to others based chiefly on the ability to purchase, display, or confer status symbols is certainly reinforced by many of society's messages, such messages will have less of an impact on people whose self-esteem is generally high. Try to determine why a deficit in your self-esteem has arisen. Did some aspect of your upbringing play a role? Should you be addressing that in some form of therapy? Is some aspect of your work life or love life contributing to your belief that you are an "unworthy" person? If so, can you do anything to gain more fulfillment in love and at work? The more you confront these core issues, the less you will feel compelled to dwell on material comparisons and to overequate money and selfhood—regardless of how much society instructs you to.

If you answered yes to any of Questions 11 to 13:

• Mitigate a low sales-resistance threshold by limiting the number of sales messages to which you are exposed. Successful advertising (successful, that is, from the advertiser's point of view, in that it gets customers to part with money) depends on both the strength of its message and the frequency with which its message is received. It *is* possible to turn down the volume during TV and radio commercials. It *is* possible to evaluate a magazine by its table of contents and thus avoid many of its ads.

• Subscribe to a reputable consumer publication that will help you distinguish between intrinsic product value and hype.

If you answered yes to any of Questions 14 to 16:

• Try to be alert to your motives for giving money or money equivalents to causes or individuals your community has designated as worthy. Are they worthy causes in *your* estimation? Give where you believe your giving can do the most good and make you feel best about giving.

• Never give more than you can comfortably spare. In the long run, giving in moderation will allow you to give more, not less.

LAYER 2: FAMILY-TRAINING-BASED RESPONSES These questions are meant to determine if your problematical money attitudes result, at least in part, from family "moneygrams."

SPOTTING A WEAK SPOT

1 Were your parents extremely secretive about money matters? Are you still in the dark regarding how much money your parents have?

2 Did your parents argue about money frequently?

3 Do you collude with any other family members to keep certain financial information from other members?

4 Do you believe you have "absorbed" a fear of poverty from your parents, though you've never been in real financial danger?

5 Do you feel like a fraud when you are in the company of your family, even if the rest of the world considers you a bona fide success?

6 Do you find yourself frequently complaining about financial mistreatment by a parent or sibling?

7 Is one of the siblings in your family the designated "success," while others seem unable or unwilling to succeed economically?

8 Do you sometimes conceptualize your financial actions (spending, saving, etc.) in terms of "being good" or "being bad"?

9 Do your parents use money to reward and punish you even now when you are an adult?

10 Do they send you money unexpectedly and expect certain prescribed gestures of affection in return?

11 Is it difficult for you to imagine outdoing your parents financially?

12 Do you frequently find yourself acting exactly the opposite way with money as your parents (e.g., do you spend flagrantly where they scrimp avidly)?

13 Was there any type of compulsive behavior in your family of origin, e.g., alcoholism, drug use, overeating?

14 Was it "understood" in your family that money was a male domain?

15 Do you notice that money is used to communicate the same emotional messages in your marriage as it did in your family of origin?

STRATEGIES

Given the amount of time we spend with our family of origin during crucial developmental years, it is inconceivable that the money lessons we learned there will have no impact on our future behavior. In many ways, the past is truly the prologue to the future where money is concerned. Responding yes to *any* of the foregoing questions indicates that the lessons you learned in the bosom of your family were not helpful ones. Here's how to begin to deactivate neurotic family money messages.

If you answered yes to any of Questions 1 to 6:

• It will be helpful to you to get more facts about your family financial life to counteract the fantasies, and to do more talking about money to counteract insidious nonverbal messages. Since your parents and siblings do not seem to be straightforward in their approach to money, try interviewing various members of your extended family to learn what you can about your immediate family through the eye of others. See what they can tell you about your forebears as well. What was the *reality* of their economic standing? How did they deal with money? Was Grandpa a tightwad; was Granny a secret spender? Many people are surprisingly ignorant of their family history before their parents' generation. Learning about the character traits and actual economic circumstances of one's grandparents and even great-grandparents can be an invaluable aid in understanding how and why certain money quirks have been passed along. There are now many books available on plotting one's own genogram (*Genograms* by Emily Marlin, a marriage and family therapist, is one I recommend), and they can be used to help you discover and conceptualize your financial family tree.

If you answered yes to Question 7:

• Compare notes with your "successful" sibling. Does he feel he received the same money messages from your parents as you did? If not, what sort of messages does he believe he received? Try *his* money messages on for size. It seems as though he feels he deserves to prosper, while you do not.

If you answered yes to Question 8:

• Instead of conceptualizing your saving and spending behaviors as "good" or "bad," ask yourself whether they are practical or impractical.

If you answered yes to Questions 9 and/or 10:

• You are being manipulated by your parents giving you money or withholding money from you. Notice what response you typically give them when they do either one of these things.

Then alter that response. By being less predictable and changing the feedback loop, you may surprise them into awareness
of their own motivations and put an end to a vicious cycle.

If you answered yes to Question 11:

• Allow yourself to visualize yourself exceeding your parents
economically. What would this feel like for you? For them?
What's really the worst that could happen? In the end, it's
unlikely they'll disown you or die of heart failure if you grow
prosperous.

If you answered yes to Question 12:

• It is your inclination to act in direct opposition to the family's primary financial trait, i.e., to overspend where they
penny-pinch or to scrimp where they are extravagant. You
must realize that in trying not to become like them you *are*
becoming like them. For you and they are given to extreme
behavior. If you really want to differentiate yourself from your
parents, try to modify your behavior toward a middle ground.

If you answered yes to Question 13:

• Be aware that any compulsive behavior in your family may
predispose you to compulsive money behaviors, e.g., compulsive spending and/or compulsive gambling. Money has many
of the same addictive properties as any chemical substance.
(Remember, researchers now believe that compulsive gamblers
actually get a physical "high" from gambling, and many a compulsive shopper has reported feeling "high" in the throes of a
shopping spree as well.) Consider attending meetings of Debtors Anonymous and/or Gamblers Anonymous, Twelve Step
Programs in the tradition of Alcoholics Anonymous, where
participants are encouraged to share their thoughts and feelings on the subject of money and are helped to regain control of

their financial lives (and, by logical extension, other aspects of their lives as well).

If you answered yes to Question 14:

• Recognize that the linkage of money and "manliness" can have detrimental effects on both sexes. Knowing what you now know about the Money Complex, it should be evident that, family and social attitudes aside, neither women nor men are born with greater inherent ability to develop laudable financial skills. (Rather, as John Spooner writes, "When it comes to money, there are very few people that have any brains at all.") Money itself has no gender preference. If you are a woman who feels "unfeminine" earning good money or managing money wisely, or a man who feels less "masculine" than others because his wallet is not as thick, you are acting on *conditioned responses.* You need to begin to deprogram yourself and seek out role models other than people in your family. Seek out women who embody your ideal of femininity, whatever that may be, and who also are not ashamed of making and having money. Seek out men who are not obsessed with material gain but evidence what you think of as "manly" qualities.

If you answered yes to Question 15:

• You have acknowledged that money is being used to fulfill the same emotional functions in your marriage as it did in the family where you were raised. Chances are thus high that you and your spouse have, like your parents before you, resorted to using money to communicate because you are unwilling to express your feelings in words. Giving verbal shape to the true nature of your grievances (e.g., "I feel you shut me out, and it makes me want to withhold from you"; or "You pay so little attention to me, I try to get you to 'pay' me in other ways") will allow you to deal with money more rationally and, overall, open the door to a stronger, healthier relationship with your spouse.

Lastly, anyone who has spotted a faulty money attitude in his family should bear this in mind:

• Most people tend to regress in periods of extreme stress and crisis. If your family is already very neurotic in its money behavior, be advised that crisis situations—sudden death, serious illness, the need to arrange nursing home care for a family member—will likely precipitate extreme regression and, thus, irrational action. To forestall utter chaos in the face of such eventualities, try to plot out a course of action ahead of time. If you don't know how to begin to think about this, consider consulting an attorney or financial planner (and select such a professional as per the criteria mentioned earlier).

LAYER I: INTRAPSYCHIC RESPONSES Answering these questions should help you discover how deep your faulty money attitudes may run. The first ten questions are meant to help you determine whether your money attitudes are, in fact, rooted in the earliest years of your life, the years when many significant character traits are shaped. The questions following are meant to help you pinpoint which, if any, of the three prevalent and primal universal money metaphors you may have appropriated for personal use: money as filth, money as food, or money as a security blanket.

SPOTTING A WEAK SPOT

1 Do you feel compelled to act a certain way toward money, even when part of yourself knows that to do so is not in your best interests?

2 Do you believe your loved ones would describe you as "inflexible" when it comes to money matters?

3 Is the first thing that comes to mind when someone suggests altering your behavior toward money the thought "I can't, I can't"?

4 Do you become enraged at people whose money-related behavior is the opposite of your own (i.e., if you are a saver, do you rail at spenders and vice versa)?

5 Do you find yourself frequently accusing others of the kind of extreme financial behavior others have accused *you* of?

6 Do you notice an extreme reluctance on your part to discuss your money or money behavior with anyone?

7 Do you believe that if people knew the truth about your financial life they wouldn't love or respect you anymore?

8 When faced with a financial problem, do you feel utterly helpless and paralyzed?

9 Do you tend to ignore financial problems until they become extremely serious?

10 Are you petrified at the thought of making any money-related decision for fear it will be the wrong one?

11 Does this trio of traits describe you: extremely frugal, exceedingly stubborn, preoccupied with order and cleanliness?

12 Do you have persistent fears that someone, somehow will manage to take your money away and "ruin" you? And are you obsessed with financial prophylaxis—taking every conceivable precaution to preserve your assets?

13 Do you feel utterly incapable of enjoying money? Do you experience feelings of shame, guilt, disgust, or disdain in connection with it?

14 Do you believe it is "wrong" to buy a luxury item even if you can easily afford it?

15 Are you extremely bitter and cynical about giving money (e.g., do you refuse to give a dollar to a homeless man because "he'll buy wine"; do you refuse to donate to charity because "the money gets stolen by bureaucrats")?

16 Or are you the polar opposite of frugal—given to spending money impulsively without much thought as to whether you really need or even want what you buy?

17 Would you call your desire for money "insatiable"?

18 Do you believe there is a certain amount of money that will provide happiness? Do you keep revising the amount upward?

19 Once you reach a financial goal you set for yourself, do you then feel let down and disappointed, as if something were missing?

20 In general, do you consider yourself an addictive personality?

21 Do infusions of money make you ebullient, while losses make you extremely forlorn?

22 Do you repeatedly find yourself in situations where you are broke or flush, with few in-betweens?

23 Do you feel much more self-possessed when you are in possession of money than when funds are low?

24 Do you experience a great deal of anxiety in relation to the comings and goings of money?

25 Do you torment yourself by conjuring up scenarios in which you envision yourself destitute and helpless?

STRATEGIES

At this level, answering affirmatively to *any* of the above questions may indicate serious money-attitude problems. And remember, attitudes at this level can be the most intractable of all. Aside from the fact that they have gelled early in life, they may also be difficult to relinquish because they sometimes bring those who hold fast to them significant secondary gains.

A money hoarder can be afforded a certain amount of pleasure from watching his pile of money swell. A compulsive spendthrift may gain intense, albeit transitory, "highs" from indulging himself and those whose admiration he hopes to garner via his own extravagance. Even someone who perceives money as a security blanket and who worries about money matters incessantly may achieve a "benefit" of sorts, in that constant money worries may serve to stave off a confrontation with deeper, darker worries such as fear of abandonment, illness, and death.

Whenever a neurosis offers a secondary gain, one's resistance to resolving it strengthens in direct proportion to that gain. Indeed, few people will want to change their behavior unless they reach a certain point—the point where the pain of *not* changing somehow begins to exceed the pain of changing. Again, when it comes to money, that point is generally reached when one's attitude toward it results in harm to one's pocketbook, damage to one's self-image and spirit, or in an inability to achieve an adequate amount of pleasure in love and at work. If any of the foregoing describes your situation, you can make a beginning at attitude revision through more in-depth attitude exploration. Here are some ways to learn more about the hidden connections and associations you may unconsciously be making to money.

If you answered yes to any of Questions 1 to 10:

• Pay attention to your compulsions. Notice when you *want* to take a new tack with money (e.g., you wish you could let yourself, for once, take a vacation with some portion of your tax refund) but feel you *must* do what you've always done in the past (e.g., put the money in the bank, like last year and the year before and the year before . . .). Pause before taking *any* action. Then imagine (just imagine) yourself engaging in the old rote behavior and imagine yourself engaging in the new original behavior. See what feelings come up for you in each scenario. What clues do they offer about your relationship to money?

• Pay attention to your *repulsions*. Notice what money behaviors in others really tend to send you "up the wall." Consider the possibility that the reason they drive you so crazy is because deep down they are so tempting to you. Consider (just consider) that you may be living your financial life in a desperate attempt to resist submitting to such impulses yourself. Ask yourself what feelings you would experience if you behaved like those whose relationship to money you criticize the most.

• Engage your unconscious as a "helper" in your attitude-revision process. It "knows" many things your conscious mind is unaware of. Before going to sleep at night, tell yourself to have a dream about money and remember it. If you indeed awake recalling such a dream, or even fragments of it, write down what you remember as soon as possible, or speak your recollections into a tape recorder (it helps to keep a pen and pad or recorder at your bedside). Think about the dream as if money were a character in it. What does this "character" want from you? What do you want from it? What emotions do you have toward it? (Be alert also to dreams featuring objects that may represent money, especially foodstuffs, transitional objects like dolls, blankets, stuffed animals, and any item that has to do with cleaning or that seems to require cleaning.)

• If you catch yourself making a slip of the tongue or of the pen when speaking or writing of money, jot down your mistake (e.g., "Wrote check for ten dollars when I meant to write a hundred" or "Told my secretary 'Don't forget petty cash owes me twenty dollars,' when I meant, 'I owe petty cash twenty dollars' "). When you have a list of such mistakes (even three or four will do), look them over and see if you can spot a pattern. What hidden urges might your mistakes indicate?

If you answered yes to one or more of Questions 11 to 15:

• Recognize that your primary emotional association to money is that *money is filth*. You may wish to reread the sections of chapter 2 entitled "Garbage and Gold" and "Anality in Action."

• Note that withholding is your main mode of action where money is concerned. You are not only withholding from others, however, you are withholding from yourself. It is, perhaps, time to ask yourself, "What is so precious that I cannot let it go?" And it is, perhaps, time to acknowledge that letting something go is often the first step in allowing yourself to get something back, something even better than that which was relinquished.

• Note that you seem to be invested in control. It is, perhaps, time to face your fears. What is the worst that could happen if you give in to spontaneity now and again? Do you believe giving up control means going out of control? That needn't be the case.

• Ask yourself, "In what other areas of my life am I given to withholding and controlling?" Addressing these areas may free you up to give up such behaviors regarding money; and, conversely, giving up such behaviors regarding money may free you to more effectively address those areas.

If you answered yes to one or more of Questions 16 to 20:

• Recognize that your primary emotional association to money is that *money is food.* You may wish to reread the section of chapter 2 entitled "Money Hungry."

• Note that consumption is your primary mode of action where money is concerned. You are not only "eating up" money in order to consume money equivalents, you are consuming all your energy in an effort to fill up an empty space inside. It is, perhaps, time to ask yourself what you are perennially missing that makes you so desperate to be temporarily sated. Feelings of being valued, of being needed, of being vibrant and alive and interested in the world around you? There are infinitely better and more long-lasting ways of availing yourself of those feelings than getting and spending money. Make a vow to do something you've always wanted to do that will net you a long-term emotional gain. Look to the areas of love and work—not to your local shopping center.

If you answered yes to one or more of Questions 21 to 25:

• Recognize that your primary emotional association to money is that *money is a security blanket*. You may wish to reread the section of chapter 2 entitled "Security Blankets and Teddy Bears."

• Note that contradictory behavior is your primary mode of action where money is concerned. You are ambivalent about whether you want money or not. You are anxious when you have it (feeling, it is likely, that you don't deserve it) and anxious when you don't (feeling, it is likely, that someone must rescue you because you are unable to help yourself). It is time to investigate why you feel so undeserving and helpless and why you use money as something to cling to in the face of those feelings. Whom did you try to cling to in the past that proved unreliable? Your mother? Your father? What did you long for that you didn't get? A stable home life? Reassuring hugs and praise? A sense of feeling consistently cared for and comforted? Ask yourself if your financial anxiety in the present may be an expression of your desire to get taken care of by those who may have disappointed you in the past. Perhaps it is time to face up to past disappointments, forgive as best you can, and move on. As it stands now, you are merely creating new opportunities for re-enacting those disappointments. Give that up, and your sense of inadequacy will diminish. You will begin to act more calmly and consistently—and not just in terms of money.

• Note also that you have a strong tendency to overidentify yourself with a sum of money. This attitude is likely to resonate in your work life and your love life, leading to superficiality in both. You may be inclined to doing work that is unfulfilling to you simply to bolster your self-esteem quotient with a hefty paycheck. You may even be prone to staying in a destructive relationship for fear that without it you will be financially bereft. This tendency, too, will diminish once you resolve to come to terms with how and why your sense of self was undermined and to set about taking steps to make yourself feel whole.

GETTING HELP

Grappling with one's money attitudes and the powerful emotions that so often underlie them is not something we may be willing or able to do all on our own. Those who wish to address issues resulting from their personal Money Complex may certainly feel in need of some sort of help.

In the strategies named in conjunction with family "moneygrams," Debtors Anonymous was mentioned specifically as a source of assistance for people dealing with a history of compulsive patterns in their family that were manifested in their own lives as a bent for compulsive spending. But some may find D.A. helpful whatever their weak spots are with regard to money. Though its name makes it sound like an organization exclusively for those whose chief problem is overdebting, D.A. also attracts a number of members who have other kinds of money problems, including those who lack the courage ever to spend anything on themselves and those who, though extremely competent, cannot seem to fulfill their earning potential.

If the idea of participating in a Twelve Step Program is of interest to you, you may wish to pick up or send for some D.A. literature and read through it to get a clearer idea of what the program entails. Or you may want to drop in at a meeting and simply listen to others speak. As someone else describes his relationship to money, you may find yourself acknowledging similar feelings you never before let yourself realize you had.

Of course, Twelve Step Programs are not for everyone.

Despite the anonymity factor, some people will find themselves unnerved at the prospect of contending with their financial/emotional problems in this sort of setting. If you are one such person, you may wish to seek another sort of assistance.

You may wish to consider therapy as a means of helping you deal with your Money Complex. But what kind of therapy should that be?

There are many kinds of therapy, some geared more than others toward in-depth psychological work. Depending on how deep one's Money Complex issues run, various approaches may prove useful in amending and adjusting one's harmful money attitudes.

Cognitive therapy operates chiefly on a conscious level. It provides people with techniques for changing the ways in which they explain their experiences to themselves. Someone who is depressed over the loss of a job, for example, may be trained through cognitive therapy to view his circumstance as an opportunity for a new beginning rather than a testament to his "failure." If one's Money Complex issues have to do with certain kinds of social issues—with, say, feeling poor because one's friends are, by comparison, more financially secure, or with feeling deprived because one cannot buy all the advertised products one desires—cognitive therapy may prove useful in offering new ways to conceptualize one's situation. Likewise, it may prove helpful in assisting people to change the way they think about investing or think about credit, provided the problems they have in those areas are primarily problems that have to do with their conscious point of view.

When money issues take their toll on family dynamics, family therapy may prove extremely useful in restoring a degree of harmony. Some family therapists have found that couples who have argued for years about money matters have never really taken the time to listen to one another's rationale for behaving the way they do. Often, the first time they listen is in the context of a therapy session—and this simple act of paying calm and respectful attention to one another's perspective may pave the way toward establishing new ground rules and compromises that are livable for both partners.

Yet while therapies that concern themselves primarily with consciously expressed conflict can clearly make some effective inroads into the Money Complex, a caveat must be mentioned. Because people do tend to regress under stress, the positive effects of such approaches may not last if deeper problems underlie difficulties at higher layers of the Complex. If, indeed, someone has a faulty money attitude grounded totally in reactions to money technology or media-generated messages, a symptom-oriented approach may resolve it once and for all. But if that attitude is merely masking a more elaborate trouble, neurotic money behavior will pop up whenever that person faces a significant enough degree of frustration, even if he has been successful at suppressing his neurosis while things in his life run more or less smoothly.

In cases where financial behaviors of husbands and wives are clearly being used to express more complicated emotional conflicts, family therapists may choose instead to work via the overt symptom, i.e., the money behavior of both partners, to affect a deep psychodynamic restructuring of the family's emotional dynamics. In *Moments of Engagement,* Dr. Peter Kramer, a psychiatrist, recounts a case he conducted in his residency training where a suggestion on his part for a radical shift of money-related behavior on the part of a wife had a profound effect on both partners' attitudes toward themselves and one another.

When this seriously depressed young woman arrived for her initial consultation, she was convinced her husband no longer loved her. Indeed, it seemed her husband had, as Kramer says, "not quite married," and one of the ways he expressed his reluctance to commit himself more completely was through money. Though he routinely turned his salary over to his wife, he put the cash income he obtained through other endeavors (a sum nearly equal to his salary) into a gambling fund. He made periodic solo trips to Las Vegas, where he was a big enough spender to merit a line of credit and a free hotel room.

When the husband confirmed to Kramer that he felt something had "gone wrong" with his wife and that she had become "too responsible" and was consumed with budget worries, the psychiatrist decided on what he terms "a paradoxical injunction." Aware that the husband was planning a gambling trip in the coming week, he instructed the wife to "go through [the husband's] private books and see how much he lost on average. She should then accompany him to Las Vegas and lose as much as [he] ordinarily did. Under no circumstances should she come back without having lost enough ... she had to learn to be frivolous."

As Kramer tells it, the wife "came back cured. She had been unable to lose all her money in the casino, so she had bought an overpriced slinky dress and strolled about, looking in on the craps tables." As for the husband, he "returned a few hundred ahead. And back in love."

Kramer's "Vegas cure" may seem, at first glance, puzzling. A marriage preserved through wanton money wasting on the part of a spouse who was formerly the more conservative of the two? Yet if one considers this case in light of what we already know about money and personal relationships, it makes a good deal of sense. By instructing the wife to assume an attitude similar to that of her husband, the psychiatrist removed the couple's barricade to the two-way street of empathy. Now the wife could allow herself to experience money as excitement and danger, a stance heretofore reserved for her husband. Now the husband could feel less compelled to act out the role of family "bad boy," in which he had used money as his principal prop. A vicious cycle was broken and a kind of emotional symmetry was restored to the relationship.

But what if someone's faulty money attitudes are based on infantile conflicts that occur as a result of breakdowns and obstructions in the early developmental process, and those breakdowns have only served to be *reinforced* at subsequent developmental stages? Then it is likely that a therapy that attempts to undo the *causes* of neurosis, i.e., psychoanalytic psychotherapy, will have the most impact.

The goal of analytic therapy is to integrate with the conscious ego the portions of the id and the superego that have been split off from the total personality. It aims to make what was unconscious conscious, and to foster the development of what is called an "observing ego" capable of instigating a reflection-before-action mode. But how so?

The analyst instructs the patient to try to the best of his ability to say anything and everything that comes to mind, without regard to sequence or "relevance" and without self-editing. But this is, of course, impossible, since in fact we edit ourselves continually. It is in noting what is omitted, i.e., in noting the various forms of *resistance* to broaching or delving into certain areas, that the analyst begins to gain an understanding of where unresolved conflicts lie.

Along with studying resistance, analysts study something called *transference*. Within the context of therapy, patients demonstrate the dynamics of their earliest significant relationships via the dynamics of the relationship they form with the analyst himself. If those early significant relationships proved troublesome in some way, those troubles will be manifested anew. In working through the problems in the therapeutic setting, the patient may finally resolve them. No longer fixated on infantile traumas, he will be free to give up repeating them over and over in his adult life in an unconscious—and therefore futile—attempt to master the hurtful emotions that were attached to them.

Because intrapsychic money metaphors are formed during infancy's preverbal period, analytic treatment—with its attention to resistance and transference—is well suited for unearthing them.

During the course of the treatment, the therapist will, in relatively short order, learn much about the patient's money attitudes by observing the myriad ways in which calm, constructive communication regarding money is resisted. (Freud speculated that civilized people are inclined to "treat matters of money as they do matters of sex, with the same inconsistency, prudishness or hypocrisy." Today, with talk of sex far more acceptable than it was in Freud's Victorian era, there exists a therapists' witticism that goes: "Some patients are more honest about what's inside their pants than inside their pants pockets.")

The therapist who employs an analytic approach will also glean a great deal about the patient's money attitudes by observing the way the patient interacts with him. A compulsive spender craves materialistic supplies as a means of offsetting a sense of inadequacy. As a rule, he craves emotional supplies as well. In his relationship with the therapist he may display excessive neediness and a constant craving for approval. He may fly into a rage or sink into glum withdrawal at the slightest sign that he is not unhesitatingly admired or when his demands for preferential treatment (e.g., for longer sessions or for excessive telephone contact) are not gratified. A compulsive hoarder, as we know, often manifests strong desires to control any given situation. He may erupt in anger if the therapist is a few minutes late in beginning a session, if office furnishings are altered in any fashion, or if the therapist should need to reschedule an appointment.

There is, of course, an obvious second window through which a therapist may gain a view of a patient's money attitudes. Therapy involves a fee, and the way in which the patient deals with the payment (or nonpayment) of that fee reveals much not only about what money may mean to the patient but about how the patient employs money to convey emotional messages—thus revealing what emotional messages were conveyed to him early on, perhaps long before he was old enough to have any idea of what money was.

Throughout the course of treatment, numerous occasions will arise for financial dealings and negotiations between patient and therapist. Such dealings can be tricky business indeed. If money matters are handled in a way that makes the patient feel misunderstood, infantilized, or pushed around, they may result in a rupture in the working alliance or even in the patient's leaving therapy. I know a young man who was billed by his therapist for a session he missed due to the sudden death of his mother. He remained outraged even after the therapist apologized profusely for what he contended was a clerical error. "I know what you fellows say about mistakes," the young man stormed. And he left treatment for good.

But despite their pitfalls, financial dealings between patient and therapist provide excellent grist for the treatment mill. They are often a way of opening the door to verbal exploration of money attitudes.

Certainly, as we are already aware, money problems are often part of larger problems, among them lack of self-esteem, lack of trust, lack of spontaneity, lack of adjustment to the reality principle, lack of true motivation at work, lack of genuine communication in relationships. There is certainly no set rule about whether financial aspects or other aspects of a problem should get addressed first. I have seen patients gain a greater sense of their own value and, as a result, demand a raise that is long overdue, or resolve an outstanding—and longstanding—debt. I have seen patients achieve greater emotional independence from their parents and, as a result, feel free to earn a great deal more money. But I have seen things work the other way around as well. A resistance to financial independence is resolved, and a whole new relationship with one's parents flowers; a more responsible attitude toward debting is assumed, and one's sense of self-worth soars.

It does not matter which comes first, the chicken or the egg. Improving one's relationship to money invariably improves one's relationship with oneself. Improving one's relationship with oneself invariably improves one's relationship to money.

TEACH YOUR CHILDREN

Of course, helping people to form rational relationships to money is not strictly a job for professionals. It is a job for parents. People who have children must take responsibility for indoctrinating them, in both the practical sense and the emotional sense, into the world of money.

Ideally, by the time one's children are old enough to contend with sophisticated money and credit instruments—checking accounts, credit cards, and the like—and with the ins and outs of investments, they should have received some practical guidance and advice from parents about fundamental concepts of finance. Thankfully, sitting one's offspring down and regaling them with a four-hour lecture on the risks of short selling and the long-term prospects for zero coupon bonds is not a mandatory requirement for responsible parenting. What's useful is to stick with the basics: How does a credit card work? What is interest? What's the difference between putting one's savings in the bank or into the stock market?

What is useful, too, is for parents to remain on the lookout for moments when a discussion of money matters can flow naturally out of the course of life's daily events. In chapter 3, an example was given of a man who used the occasion of a family outing to Washington's Air and Space Museum to introduce his daughter to the idea of a "loan." Such opportunities for impromptu financial lessons present themselves all the time.

An acquisitive child, in urgent need of extra money for a Nintendo game, a Bart Simpson T-shirt, or a double Whopper with cheese, may request an advance on his allowance or ask for permission to raid his piggy bank. Here's a chance to introduce the concepts of "debt" and "capital." An inquisitive child may poke his nose into a parent's papers when checking accounts are being balanced or tax returns being prepared, asking, "What are you doing?" All right, this may not be the ideal time for a lengthy chat, but it is a chance to begin to explain briefly that certain tasks are a requisite part of dealing with money responsibly and rationally—and perhaps to set a time, after your paperwork is accomplished, for discussing and demonstrating some of the basics.

The more simply and nonthreateningly that basic financial concepts can be explained, the greater the chance that a child will in later years deal with money matters in a state of relative calm. With children—and with adults, too, for that matter—visual aids and analogy tend to go a lot further than off-putting jargon. The father at the Air and Space Museum tore bits off a plain sheet of paper to demonstrate the way loan repayment worked. Anything that's handy and that can be easily broken down into smaller pieces—building blocks, oranges, pieces of chalk—can be used to demonstrate the workings of money and credit and the principles of investing. And any family that has a computer can probably find ways of using *it* to make learning about money interesting and fun.

A pleasant introduction to something in childhood can do much to alleviate later life anxieties about whatever that thing may be. As we know, children who enjoy learning to swim tend to be, for all time, unafraid to jump into the water. Thus, simply to convey via one's teaching techniques the message that money need not be a source of fear and frustration is to lay constructive emotional groundwork for a child's long-term money attitudes.

To engender the truly healthiest possible money attitudes in one's children, however, parents must address money's emotional elements in many other ways as well. For one thing, it falls to parents to balance out detrimental social money messages that stress achieving parity with one's peers through getting and spending.

Children find peer acceptance extremely important, and there is little harm, and doubtless some good, in occasional capitulations to their demands that they be bought something because "all the other kids have one"—provided the parents can really afford what is desired. But even parents who could, at least in theory, afford to meet all their children's demands for status-related objects would do well in practice to resist some anyhow, with a loving but firm explanation that a line is being drawn to prevent overemphasis on material things. Giving in to a child's every such whim will serve only to lend credence to the misbegotten notion that the essence of someone's worth—not just other people's but his own—lies in the things he has and how much those things cost.

It falls also to parents to be as alert as possible to the ways money is used to communicate emotional messages in the home. Is one child financially feted while another is, relatively speaking, financially famished? If so, both children may grow up to act irrationally toward money.

Are you and your spouse using money to control each other, test each other, tease or torment each other? If so, you had best figure out just what the underlying problem is in your relationship and address it directly. If you do not, you will *without a doubt* instill in your children a bent for employing money to express emotions that would be far less damaging if put into words. Are you and your partner continually quarreling about money? If so, you are in danger of raising full-fledged money avoiders who associate the mere mention of the word with tension and misery.

Does your family perpetuate traditions that convey the message that money is a male domain? If so, you may be raising sons who will not feel like "real men" unless they are pursuing money above all else. And you may be raising daughters who will not feel like "real women" unless they are financially dependent (perhaps on *you*).

But when it comes to shaping the money attitudes of one's children, perhaps the most important of the emotional tasks that fall to parents involve the ways in which they deal with those children as people, from infancy onward. Babies in bassinets know nothing of dollars, but they know when they feel gratified or frustrated, comforted or thwarted, cared for or neglected. Toddlers in toilet training know when their efforts are met with praise versus silence, and when their mistakes are greeted with reassurance versus condemnation. And children of all ages know when they are held in high regard by their parents, when they are respected and admired, rather than manipulated and demeaned.

Those who grow up feeling valued will value themselves. They will be less prone to envy, to anxiety, and to ambivalence. They will be more inclined to be generous, but not to the point where they undermine themselves. They will be inclined to be original rather than rigid, but not to be impulsive or rash. They will tend to have a moral sense and a socially appropriate conscience, but not to fall prey to self-destructive guilt and shame. And as a result of all this, they will be, most assuredly, less prone—not immune, but less prone—to money madness.

THE "LAWS" OF MONEY

It is not likely that any of us, no matter how hard we try, will ever be able to completely eradicate the Money Complex, either in ourselves or in the children we raise. The way in which money both influences and reflects our life stories places a limit on the amount of financial objectivity we can ultimately achieve. But just because we may never behave like paragons of sanity when it comes to money does not mean we have to let it make us *in*sane. And just because we cannot operate with utter objectivity does not mean we cannot operate with a healthy amount of decisiveness and thoroughness, flexibility and imagination, judiciousness, confidence, and competence.

It was said earlier that it is difficult to conceive of many absolute truths about something so paradoxical as money. But many things are paradoxical, and still we find we do tend to do best if we devise for ourselves a set of truths to live by and stick with them in the absence of anything better. The nature of the universe is a paradox, but we inhabit the earth and explore our solar system according to the "laws" of physics as we conceptualize them. There are, in the same sense, "laws" of money too.

• Money is neither god nor devil. But in this world it is a necessity.

• Money can be used constructively or destructively.

• Money can symbolize anything we wish it to.

• Much of the way we behave toward money is unconsciously motivated.

• Money is safest when it is "out of the closet," discussed calmly and candidly with one's spouse, one's parents, and, most especially, one's children.

• A degree of detachment from money is desirable. A disdain for money is detrimental.

• In order to have enough money so that one does not have to think about it, one must think about it.

• Those who feel they don't deserve to have much money usually don't.

• Those who will not share some of their money suffer emotional and social consequences.

• Those who only take and do not "make" money suffer emotional and social consequences.

• Where money is given there is expectation.

• Where money is taken there is obligation.

• Love goes better when partners know that love is not money.

• Work goes better when money is a by-product *of* work and not the principal motivation *to* work.

• We are not what we earn, own, or owe. We are what we are.

And lastly:

• Money is not time. Time is time.

About this last "law," a bit more must be said. For, after all, a certain number of pages have already been devoted to exploring similarities between time and money and ways in which our minds are inclined to link the two. But mostly we think of time's equivalence to money when we are thinking in terms of work done for money. For it is true that we can convert life energy into money. But alas, it doesn't work the other way around.

Life is lived at its fullest when it is lived in the moment, when, free of self-consciousness and anxiety, we are wholly absorbed in transcendent acts—acts of creation and of procreation, acts of meditation and deep contemplation, acts of intense physical exertion, acts of exaltation, acts of love. Money is never about the moment. Yes, it is about the past, in that it is an inextricable element of personal and social history. Yes, it is about the present, in the sense of the day-to-dayness of money concerns. And yes, it is about the future, in that it necessitates planning ahead. But money plays no part in the best parts of life, in the parts where we experience ourselves as part of something beyond ourselves.

If we plan wisely, we may never run out of money. We may even be "rich" as the eighteenth-century British historian Edward Gibbon defined rich—one with an income superior to one's expense and expense equal to one's wishes. But no matter what we plan or hope, we will all, at least as far as our earthly existence goes, run out of time.

The late Jack Benny never failed to draw his biggest laugh in a vaudeville bit where a hold-up man sticks a gun in his ribs and says, "Your money or your life." Benny would take a beat. Then another. And another. Finally he'd scratch his head. "I'm thinking," he'd say. "I'm thinking."

Benny's comic genius lay in knowing just how long to wait before responding to the gunman. As the tension that is a prelude to laughter built, his audience began to get the picture. Could it be . . . could it be he is actually making a *choice*? When the laugh comes, it is so intense precisely because no one watching really believes he himself would make such a choice. It's hilarious—absurd!—to imagine anyone surrendering his life in the face of such a rhetorical threat. Much easier to imagine surrendering the wallet. Indeed, much easier to imagine someone gasping with a dying breath, as did Queen Elizabeth I, "All my possessions for a moment of time."

Much as we are preoccupied with money, much as we know, or should know, that a portion of our lives must be given over to its demands, we know, or should know, that the real bottom line is not about money after all. And we sense that the truest of truths to live by is this rather famous tale, told in the fifth century B.C. by the Greek historian Herodotus:

> Croesus, the richest of kings, approached Solon, the Athenian lawgiver and sage, asking who was the happiest of mortals. Solon replied that in seventy years, which he regarded as the limit of a man's life-time, there are, counting intercalary months, 26,250 days, not one producing events like the rest. "For yourself, Croesus," he said, "I see that you are wonderfully rich . . . but with respect to your question, I have no answer to give, until I hear that you have closed your life happily."

Notes on Sources

INTRODUCTION

John Kenneth Galbraith's quote can be found in the introduction to *Money: Whence It Came, Where It Went* (Boston: Houghton Mifflin, 1975).

CHAPTER I

The first epigraph to this chapter is from *Soul and Money* by Russell A. Lockhart, James Hillman et al. (Dallas: Spring Publications, Inc., 1982). The second epigraph is from *The Philosophy of Andy Warhol: From A to B and Back Again*, edited by Pat Hackett (New York: Harcourt Brace Jovanovich, 1975). The New York Federal Reserve Bank, which gives tours if telephone reservations are made a week in advance, is only one of many Federal Reserves around the nation. In total, the Reserve banks shred some $200 million of unusable currency a day. The University of Pennsylvania experiment is cited by Mark Zussman in "The Psychology of Money" (*Fairmont* magazine, Volume 2, Number 2). The Gallup Poll referred to was a 1987 study entitled "The No Nonsense Women's Attitude Survey." The German banker's suicide note was quoted by John Spooner in *Sex and Money* (Boston: Houghton Mifflin, 1985). "We're in the Money," a song written by Harry Warren in 1933 and sung in the musical *Forty-Second Street*, although popularly known by this title, was originally titled "The Gold Diggers' Song."

CHAPTER 2

The *Wall Street Journal* story on Igloo, South Dakota, reported by Ken Wells, appeared on November 28, 1988. Freud's "Character and Anal Eroticism" (1908) appears in Volume 9 of the Standard Edition.

Don Henley's song "If Dirt Were Dollars" appears on his 1989 album *The End of the Innocence*. The coin-polishing practices at the Pacific Union Club were described in Lewis Lapham's *Money and Class in America* (New York: Weidenfeld & Nicolson, 1988). The Karl Abraham essay referred to is "Contributions to the Theory of the Anal Character" (1921). Charles Higham's biography is entitled *The Duchess of Windsor: The Secret Life* (New York: McGraw-Hill, 1988). Otto Fenichel's "The Drive to Amass Wealth" was published in 1934. An article about George Bush's golden truffles, "Gold's an Acquired Taste," appeared on *USA Today*'s front page on November 23, 1988. The cited information on pig hormones is from a front-page *Wall Street Journal* article, "Pigs May Provide Hints for Humans on Not Being Hogs" (December 8, 1988). Melanie Klein's quote is from her paper "A Study of Envy and Gratitude" (1956). Imelda Marcos's statements were reported by *Business Week*, December 15, 1988. The *New York* magazine column item on Al Neuharth's retirement luncheon ran in the April 10, 1989, issue.

CHAPTER 3

The epigraph to this chapter is from *Trump: The Art of the Deal* by Donald J. Trump with Tony Schwartz (New York: Random House, 1987). The case of the rich banker's lesson to his children can be found in Karl Abraham's "Contributions to the Theory of the Anal Character" initially cited in chapter 2. The theory of cognitive dissonance, i.e., the concept that two contrary "truths" cannot coexist in an individual's mind, was originated by social psychologist Leon Festinger. A Yankelovich Clancy Shulman survey which appeared in *New Woman*'s October 1990 issue revealed that in many instances the more men earn the more masculine they feel. Men who say they feel "more masculine" than others earn more money than their counterparts who say they feel "as masculine" as other men, or less so.

CHAPTER 4

The epigraph to this chapter is from John Kenneth Galbraith's *Money: When It Came, Where It Went* (op. cit.). The *New York Times* article "Isolated Desert Community Lives by Skinner's Precepts" (November 7, 1989) was reported by Larry Rohter. Should teachers choose to supplement School Savings literature, a host of other educational tools are currently available. Nowadays, junior high and high school students may further their economic knowledge by playing the Stock Market Game, created by the Securities Industry Association (competing teams invest a hypothetical $100,000 and see whose choices prove the most lucrative) and the Chicago Board of Trade's Commodity Challenge (students are judged on the validity of their reasons for moving in and out of markets). The results of the ABC News quiz on the economy were discussed by Ted Koppel on "A National Town Meeting on Wall Street and the Economy," an edition of "Nightline" which aired November 6, 1987. Tom Wolfe's quote appeared in a *Time* magazine interview, "Master of His Universe" (February 13, 1989). Carlton Wagner's theories on color are discussed on his videotape "The Psychology of Color." See also the *New York* magazine article "Color Schemes" (April 3, 1989), in which Wagner is extensively quoted. The quotes from Jimmy Swaggart and Jim Bakker appeared in *Ministry of Greed* by Larry Martz (New York: Weidenfeld & Nicolson, 1988). Marvin Harris's quote is from his book *Our Kind* (New York: Harper & Row, 1989).

CHAPTER 5

The first epigraph to this chapter is from Adam Smith's April 1988 *Esquire* column. The second is from Fernand Braudel's *Civilization and Capitalism, 15th–18th Century* (New York: Harper & Row, 1981). The *New York Times* art review by Rita Reif was entitled "It May Look Like a Hoe, but It's Really Money" (October 30, 1988). Andy Warhol's thoughts on checks and cash can be found in *The Philosophy of Andy Warhol* (op. cit.). Fernand Braudel's quotes are from *Civilization and Capitalism, 15th–18th Century* (op. cit.). *Money*'s article on tax advice, "The Pros Flunk Our New Tax-Return Test," reported by Greg Anrig, Jr., appeared in the March 1989 issue. "Watch Your Assets," by Janet Bamford and William G. Flanagan appeared in the October 8, 1984, issue of *Forbes*. Credit card collector Walter Cavanagh's exploits were reported in the *San Francisco Chronicle* in the article "The No. 1 Credit Card Collector" by Sharon McCormick (August 27, 1989). The *New York Times* article "Is the Deficit Really a Threat? Maybe Not, Some Are Saying" (January 23, 1989) was reported by Peter Kilborn. The *Business Week* article on Harunori Takahashi, "Meet the World's Busiest Man—Oops, You Missed Him," appeared in the April 17, 1989, issue.

CHAPTER 6

Charles Mackay's chronicle of "tulipomania" can be found in *Extraordinary Popular Delusions and the Madness of Crowds*, originally published in 1841, it was later reprinted (New York: Harmony Books, 1980). The book also contains chapters on the Mississippi Scheme and the South Sea Bubble. William McDougall, author of *The Group Mind* (Cambridge: 1920), is quoted in Sigmund Freud's *Group Psychology and the Analysis of the Ego* (1921). LeBon's *The Crowd: A Study of the Popular Mind* (London: 1920) was originally published in Paris, in 1895, as *Psychologie des Foules*. It was Jean Piaget who showed that representational thinking was impossible for children before age six. For more information, see Piaget's *The Construction of Reality in the Child* (New York: Basic Books, 1954). George Washington's quote was found in *Coins and Currency*, an information pamphlet published by the Federal Reserve. The information on parents' instructions to children during Brazil's inflation was written about by Charles Kuralt in *A Life on the Road* (New York: Putnam, 1990). John Russell's *New York Times* article was entitled "Clapping for Money at Auctions" (May 21, 1989). The story behind Alan Bond's purchase of *Irises* can be found in the *New York Times* article "Vincent Van Gogh, Meet Adam Smith" (February 4, 1990). The *New York Times* interview with John J. Phelan, Jr., "Big Board's John J. Phelan Jr. Looks at the Plunge and Beyond," appeared on October 27, 1987. Ted Koppel's interview with Dr. Jay Rohrlich aired on ABC's "Nightline" on November 6, 1987. Dr. Robert Schiller's quote is from the article "Dow and Reason: Distant Cousins?" *The New York Times* (August 25, 1989). Dr. James Ramsey's quote is from "When Chaos Rules the Market," *The New York Times* (November 22, 1987). The University of Michigan study involving racetrack betting was cited in *Newsweek's* "The Market on the Couch" (November 2, 1987). Jack Dreyfus was quoted in *Time* (July 25, 1960). The unnamed media consultant's quote on Michael Milken appeared in the *Vanity Fair* article "The Man Who Fell to Earth" (August 1989). Jane Bryant Quinn's statement was made on the aforementioned edition of ABC's "Nightline." Isaac Asimov's *Skeptical Inquirer* quote was cited by John Allen Paulos in *Innumeracy* (New York: Hill and Wang, 1988). The Rothschild quote is from *Fallen Angels, High Steppers and Lollipops* (New York: Dodd, Mead, 1988). Adam Smith's description of Ben Graham's principles can be found in *The Roaring '80s* (New York: Summit, 1988).

CHAPTER 7

Edmund Bergler's quote is from his book *Money and Emotional Conflicts* (New York: Doubleday, 1951). The faulty thinking of gamblers is reviewed in Dr. Willem A. Wagenaar's book *Paradoxes of Gambling Behavior* (Lawrence Erlbaum Associates, 1989). The Yale Primate experiment was cited in Mark Zussman's article "The Psychology of Money" (op. cit.). Nelson Aldrich's quote on work is from *Old Money* (New York: Knopf, 1988). Recent research on the phenomenon of "flow" is chronicled in *The New York Times Magazine* article "The Power of Concentration" (October 8, 1989). The *Fortune* quote on Bill Gates appeared in the October 1987 "Billionaires" issue.

CHAPTER 8

David Michaelis's "The Nutcracker Suit" appeared in the December 1984 issue of *Manhattan, inc.*

CHAPTER 9

The second epigraph is a quote from Michael Lewis's *Liar's Poker* (New York: Norton, 1989). The information of the Office of Currency Standards is from a *New York Times Magazine* article, "No Money in the Microwave, Please" (December 10, 1989). John Allen Paulos's quote is from *Innumeracy* (New York: Hill and Wang, 1988). The Veblen quote is from *The Theory of the Leisure Class* (New York: Macmillan, 1899). Laura Rockefeller's quote appeared in Vance Packard's *The Ultra-Rich* (Boston: Little, Brown, 1989). *Genograms* by Emily Marlin is published by Contemporary Books, Chicago, 1989. John Spooner's quote is from *Sex and Money* (op. cit.). For the complete account of the "Vegas cure" see the chapter "Is Empathy Necessary?" in Peter Kramer's *Moments of Engagement* (New York: Norton, 1989). Solon's quote is from Daniel J. Boorstin's *The Discoverers* (New York: Vintage, 1985).

Index

About the Author

ARLENE MODICA MATTHEWS is a pyschotherapist in private practice in New York City. She also leads group workshops and seminars on the subject of money and emotions. She has appeared many times on national television and her articles have appeared in numerous publications, including *Money* magazine. Her previous book, *Why Did I Marry You, Anyway?*, helped couples grapple with adjustments to marriage—including financial adjustments. She lives in Manhattan with her husband.